Love Every Leaf

Published in Canada by Tundra Books,
75 Sherbourne Street, Toronto, Ontario M5A 2P9

Published in the United States by Tundra Books of Northern New York,
P.O. Box 1030, Plattsburgh, New York 12901

Library of Congress Control Number: 2007927433

Library and Archives Canada Cataloguing in Publication
Stinson, Kathy
Love every leaf : the life of landscape architect Cornelia Hahn
Oberlander / Kathy Stinson.

Includes bibliographical references.
ISBN 978-0-88776-804-0

1. Oberlander, Cornelia Hahn--Juvenile literature.
2. Landscape architects--Canada--Biography--Juvenile literature.
3. Holocaust survivors--Canada--Biography--Juvenile literature.
I. Title.

SB470.O23S75 2008   j712.092   C2007-902734-2

We acknowledge the financial support of the Government of Canada through the Book Publishing
Industry Development Program (BPIDP) and that of the Government of Ontario through the
Ontario Media Development Corporation's Ontario Book Initiative.

We further acknowledge the support of the Canada Council for
the Arts and the Ontario Arts Council for our publishing program. ONTARIO ARTS COUNCIL
CONSEIL DES ARTS DE L'ONTARIO

Printed in the United States of America

1 2 3 4 5 6   13 12 11 10 09 08

Love Every Leaf

The Life of Landscape Architect Cornelia Hahn Oberlander

Kathy Stinson

TUNDRA BOOKS

Dedicated to

Humphrey Carver, my late father-in-law and co-founder
of the Canadian Society of Landscape Architects.

Table of Contents

"We don't show children enough of what is beautiful."

– *Cornelia Oberlander*

The Author Meets Her Subject

When I first met Cornelia in 2004, all I knew about her was that an article in *Gardening Life* magazine had called her "The Grand Dame: A design legend with staying power" and that her husband, Peter Oberlander, used to work with my late father-in-law. When Peter heard that my husband was going to be in Vancouver, he suggested that they get together for lunch, and that Cornelia and I come along.

Cornelia, age four, in her childhood garden in Germany, and more recently in her Vancouver home-studio.

As we approached the Oberlander's house, a hemlock hedge blocked our view of the garden – until we passed through an arch cut into the dense branches. Then a pathway of flat stones led us past a mossy lawn, some ferns, clumps of wild grasses, azaleas, periwinkle, and lily of the valley, to the heavy wood front door. Designed by Peter, their house balanced comfortably on two steel pillars, like stilts, at the edge of a wooded ravine.

Peter led my husband and me to the living room. The entire back wall (all glass) faced a sea of green. Two enormous rhododendrons, about 26 feet (8 m) tall, grew close to the window. The house itself was filled with all kinds of interesting things: Inuit carvings, paintings, a garden shovel hanging on one wall, and books – about Hong Kong bamboos, Alberta's parks, plants of the Vancouver region, Frederick Law Olmsted, healing plants used by West Coast Indians. . . .

When Cornelia swept into the room, she seemed tall, but in fact she is no more than 5 foot 2 (160 cm). (I would later learn that before she was even eight years old, one of her teachers, Fraulein Pufahl, held a ruler against her spine as she walked to encourage good posture.)

We went to the Faculty Club at the University of British Columbia (UBC) for lunch. From a balcony overlooking a large green space, Cornelia described a nearby area she had designed, and expressed her disappointment that a mound had been planted with many kinds of shrubs instead of the low-lying groundcover she had wanted. (She felt that the shrubs cluttered the smooth, rolling line of the mound.) Elsewhere, a rose garden had not been built at the proper slope to give people the chance to walk around it and discover the buds and blooms from different angles, as she had wished. Over lunch, Cornelia told me how she had come to know when she was only eleven years old that she wanted to be a landscape architect.

Thinking I'd like to read about this interesting woman, I asked if anyone had ever written a biography of her.

"No," she answered, "and no one who has ever written about me has ever quite got me." She looked at me then and said, "Perhaps *you'll* be the one."

I smiled politely but to myself dismissed the idea. I'd never written biography before, I was busy with other writing projects, and Cornelia was probably kidding anyway. But after a brief tour of some of the spaces she had designed at UBC, and after reading an envelope of articles she thrust into my hand when we returned to the Oberlander house, I was hooked.

When the folks at Tundra Books were enthusiastic too, Cornelia was thrilled. But when I began to explore aspects of her life only briefly covered in the articles, she bristled. In a no-nonsense and suspicious tone of voice, she said, "I thought you were depicting me as a landscape architect." Even pinning down her birth date (surely the first bit of information a biographer must have!) was not straightforward.

"Cornelia," I said, "in the brief account you have given me of your life in Germany, I found your parents' birth dates and your sisters' birth dates, but not yours."

"I'll get you that later."

Couldn't she just *tell* me when she was born? I didn't push, and a few minutes later she came back to it. "My birth was June 20, 1924. I am ancient by now."

"June 20, 1924," I repeated slowly, and even though I was recording our interview, I made a point of writing it down. "Okay . . . now . . . I did see that date in the Canadian Encyclopedia."

"Mhm." Was she advising me to drop the subject, or daring me to continue?

I continued. "But . . . when I was putting together dates in the little bio you gave me, I worked you out as having . . . a different birthday."

"Well, in truth, yes," she answered. "But that is the official one. Okay?"

I laughed. Did she really think I could write her biography and give an "official" but *false* date of birth? "Okay, but . . . how is it that you have two birthdays?"

"I don't know," she said. "What are we going to do about that?" She then confessed that she was born in 1921. When I said that's what I'd thought, she said, "Leave it then. 1921. Straighten me out."

At times Cornelia seemed to trust me; other times she spoke guardedly. Gradually I realized that she was pleased I was writing a book about her only because she saw it as a way of having more people understand the work she and other landscape architects do, and of perhaps inspiring young people to enter the profession. "Don't think so much about my life," she said. "Think about being a catalyst for ideas. Write something and elevate us all."

Cornelia Oberlander, who has been a landscape architect for more than sixty years, considers landscape architecture "the art of the possible." I've come to believe that "the art of the possible" also defines the very way this remarkable woman lived her life.

– *Kathy Stinson*

Chapter One

An Enchanted Garden

Where were they hiding? On the other side of that bed of flowers? The little girl ran to see. Butterflies flitted among the blossoms, but no one else was there. She ran across the lawn to a grove of trees where she sometimes liked to hide, even when she wasn't playing games with her younger sister and cousin. Surrounded by green, it was her favorite place to look at a book, listen to birds chirping, or imagine being an ant crawling over an ant hill.

No one was hiding in her grove of trees, but something rustled at the far end of the garden. Her cousin, giving himself away? The girl ran – past the pond, today reflecting puffy white clouds and blue sky – toward the bushes. When she crawled between the shrubs, a rabbit scampered out and away. Cornelia laughed, and again all was still.

Maybe someone was hiding between the purple lilac – her favorite bush in the garden – and the gate to the street.

The bush smelled wonderful, but no, neither Charlotte nor Oscar was hiding there. Would they have gone outside the gate? Cornelia opened it and peeked out. Her friend Jutta was walking down the Bernhard Beyerstrasse with her father.

"Have you seen my sister?" Cornelia called.

Beate Hahn introduces her infant daughter Cornelia to her first garden. The playhouse (opposite) was later taken down and reassembled in the United States.

5

Jutta, whose father was a doctor, had not seen her.

Cornelia's own father, an engineer, was in the United States on business. Cornelia's mother, a horticulturalist, was well known for her children's books about gardening. Other people in Cornelia's family were pretty accomplished, too. Her great-grandfather established the *Hahn'sche Werke*, a business for manufacturing seamless pipes, which he had invented. Her grandmother founded a housing association to clean up slums in Berlin. Her Uncle Kurt would found the survival skills education organization called Outward Bound. Her Uncle Otto was a brilliant scientist who would one day win a Nobel Prize in chemistry. Only seven years old, Cornelia didn't know what she would be when she grew up.

Back in the garden, she couldn't think where Charlotte and Oscar could be hiding, so she decided to check on her vegetable patch. Each year when the green shoots emerged from the ground, it was like a magical surprise all over again. Cornelia pulled a weed from between the rows of corn and pea plants, then went to climb a tree.

From here she could see the shingled rooftops of houses along the street and not far away the lush green forest. Should she go see if her sister and cousin were hiding there, or just stay where the lovely patterns of sunlight and shadows flickered along the thick branch that held her?

Just then, Cornelia heard giggling. She looked up. And there were Charlotte and Oscar – perched on branches above her head.

"I didn't think *you* could get up here!" she shouted and then laughed. This garden was the best place in the world and this tree the best hiding place.

Cornelia was too young to be aware that a dark cloud was hanging over that garden. It was 1928, and Adolf Hitler was busy convincing the German people that "the Jews" were to blame for all the country's problems. Before long, many Jewish people would be looking desperately for places to hide, and it would be no game. But on that sunny day when Cornelia smelled the lilacs and climbed a copper beech, no one knew the devastation Hitler's policies would soon bring to peaceful gardens throughout the country – and to the world beyond.

How did a man like Hitler come to have so much power that he could succeed in having large numbers of the country's population exterminated?

After World War I ended (in 1919), Germany was in bad shape. In the 1920s, its money was next to worthless. Can you imagine buying a loaf of bread or a soft drink for $1 one summer, and having to pay $6 for it the next? That's what happened between June 1921, when Cornelia was born, and June 1922. From July to November of 1923, prices increased again by somewhere between a million and a billion times their previous level. Even if you were lucky enough to have a wheelbarrow full of money, it would buy you practically nothing. When the Great Depression hit countries such as the United States that had lent money to Germany years earlier, these countries asked Germany to repay the loans because they needed that money now. The German economy came close to collapse.

Adolf Hitler saw the crumbling economy as a chance to gain political power. It wasn't hard to convince people that Jews were to blame for the country's problems because many wealthy business owners were Jewish. And with his detailed plan for eliminating unemployment, it was easy to seduce people who were hungry for jobs. Many of the jobs Hitler created were in the construction of the Autobahn, a substantial system of roads that would one day help move troops effectively across the country.

When Hitler's plans to improve the economy succeeded, his rise to power was all but assured. Under his dictatorship, all forms of democratic government and any opposition to his policies were swept away. His Nazi Party pledged to restore Germany to its "rightful place" in Europe, and to wipe all Jewish people from the face of the earth.

Kathy Stinson

Chapter Two

Germany's Noxious Weed

Cornelia, at thirteen, in her riding outfit in front of the family home in Neubabelsberg-Wannsee, a suburb of Berlin.

Cornelia was home-schooled until she was eight years old. When she went to school, she was hardly aware that she was one of only a few Jewish children there.

When Cornelia was eleven years old and still oblivious to what was going on in the world around her, her mother took her to an artist's studio to have her portrait painted. She would rather have been riding her horse, climbing trees, or swimming in Lake Wannsee, but since before her great-great-grandmother's time, it had been a family tradition that every girl should have her portrait done before she turned twelve.

Sitting with her back straight and her hands folded in her lap, Cornelia sighed. Would the painter never finish? It was warm inside the studio. The collar of her dress chafed her neck. Glancing sideways – she knew she mustn't turn her head – Cornelia studied a mural on the north wall of the studio. A winding river was colored blue. Meeting the river at right angles was a gridiron pattern of beige-colored streets.

"What are the red boxes in that drawing?" Cornelia asked.

The artist, with her eye on the girl's fair hair, dipped her brush into a blob of light yellow paint. "Those are houses."

"And the green areas?"

8

"They are parks."

Cornelia liked the irregular green shapes scattered around the drawing. When she arrived home from the studio, she told her mother, "When I grow up, I'm going to make parks."

Her mother said, "You want to be a landscape architect."

"Yes."

"That's a difficult job." Since landscape architects in Germany at that time also ran construction companies, her mother added, "And you will have to drive a bulldozer."

Cornelia didn't miss a beat. "Good!"

🌿

By the end of 1932, Cornelia's parents were growing concerned about Hitler's rising power. On New Year's Eve, her father made her mother promise they'd leave Germany, and soon.

Twelve days later, he was killed in an avalanche while skiing. Cornelia lay in bed, numb, but her mother insisted she get up. Yes, Papa was dead, but life must go on. The family would even continue to go on skiing holidays in Switzerland, just as they had before. "He could as easily have died crossing a street," her mother said. "You can't stop living."

Two weeks after the tragic death of her father, Cornelia hurried in from the cold. Her mother was talking to the cook about whether to have roast beef or lamb for dinner. Before going to her room to work on the next chapter of a new book, she said, "Today President Hindenburg made Hitler Chancellor." Cornelia didn't know exactly

Cornelia and her father ham it up on their skis while on holiday in Switzerland. The Hahns continued to take skiing holidays, even after Cornelia's father was killed in an avalanche.

Kathy Stinson

9

what that meant, but she knew it wasn't good.

Determined to keep life as normal as possible, Mrs. Hahn allowed her daughters to continue English and French lessons and to go swimming in Lake Wannsee. Cornelia learned to ride dressage and do circus work on a horse inherited from Jewish friends who were emigrating. Mrs. Hahn arranged musical events for Cornelia and her younger sister to take part in – a performance of *Wirbauen eine neue stadt* (We are building a new city), an opera by Hindemith, and Haydn's *Kinder Symphony*. Not musically talented, Cornelia played the triangle.

By the time Cornelia went to high school, there were no other Jewish girls in her class because many Jewish families had already emigrated. It was not unusual, throughout Germany, to hear cries of "Heil Hitler!" and to see the Nazi salute. In 1935, to exert even more control over citizens, the Nazis began burning books. Still Cornelia's mother was confident that her daughter would not run into problems with Nazi officers as she rode the six miles (10 km) to school on her bicycle. But as time went on, it became more and more difficult to ignore the fact that the Nazi regime was changing how they lived.

One Sunday in 1935, four officers of the most powerful Nazi organization in Germany came to the Hahn's home. They wore high, shining, black boots. Their faces expressionless, they pushed into the dining room where the family was eating. They insisted on inspecting the kitchen, too, for evidence that the Hahns might be breaking a new law that dictated that once a month everyone must eat a one-pot soup – *ein Topfpericht* – instead of their usual Sunday dinner. If the Hahns were eating roast beef, or anything else they were used to having before the new law was passed, the officers would have an excuse to arrest them.

Throughout the ominously quiet ordeal, Cornelia held her breath, asking herself over and over how this could be happening. The family had done nothing wrong and was hardly even Jewish. They celebrated Hanukkah, but they had a Christmas tree, too.

But it was happening. The smell of the officers' uniforms was in the house, the marks of their boot heels on the floor, and Cornelia was terrified.

Finally the officers finished their inspection. Cornelia's mother politely asked them to leave.

❧

When Cornelia was fifteen she could run – faster than all the other girls. With her school's Sports Day coming, she could hardly wait to take home the prize for the 100-meter dash. The day before the event Mrs. Hahn received a phone call from the teacher. Cornelia would not be allowed to participate. No explanation was given and none was necessary.

From then on, Cornelia no longer attended school. She spent her time learning at home, riding her horse, King, and working in the garden.

One day, her friend Jutta's younger brother told a group of children, "My father doesn't like Hitler." One of the boys told his parents what Jutta's brother had said, and soon after, Jutta's father, a Jewish doctor, disappeared.

It was time for the Hahns to get out of Germany.

Kathy Stinson

Can you find eleven-year-old Cornelia in this class photo?

Chapter Three

Expulsion from the Garden

On her sixteenth birthday, June 20, 1937, Cornelia was still in Germany. She received a letter from her grandmother, who had been taking her to museums since she was six. Written in the form of a poem, the letter predicted that Cornelia would some day make beautiful gardens, "with columns covered with clematis, summer houses surrounded by roses, and little rivers trickling over stones. And you will have thought of all this out of thousands of remembrances . . . Every thing you have contact with will be woven into your garden . . . What you have created with the blood of your heart will be remembered by future generations." Cornelia's grandmother was putting into her own words something written by a Japanese noble for creators of gardens in the eleventh century, words that would later guide Cornelia, too:

> Begin by considering the lay of the land and water. Study the work
> of past masters, and recall the places of beauty that you know.
> Then, on your chosen site, let memory speak, and make into your
> own that which moves you most.

It was a loving letter from a grandmother to a granddaughter she knew would be leaving her soon, but getting out of Germany was becoming a tricky

The wooden Noah's ark with hand-carved animals (above) was one of Cornelia's favorite toys as a young girl. Opposite, a grown-up Cornelia and her mother, Beate Hahn, enjoy the Swiss sunshine.

13

business. Cornelia's family was still in the country on November 9th, 1938, when the Nazis rampaged through the streets of Berlin destroying Jewish homes and businesses. The Hahns lived far enough from the center of the city that Cornelia did not witness what came to be known as *Kristallnacht* – the "Night of Broken Glass" – when the Nazis burned one hundred and ninety-one synagogues and arrested twenty thousand Jews. But her sister, being driven to a piano lesson, did. When Charlotte got to her lesson, her teacher – who was Jewish – was not there. Had he been seized by the Nazis? She would never know.

The Hahns knew that the Nazis could come to their home again at any time and seize their passports. Cornelia suggested taking them to the American Consulate for safekeeping.

Around the consulate on Bellevuestrasse, people were lined up three rows deep, waiting to be given numbers that would determine when they would be allowed to leave Germany. It would take months for many of those numbers to come up because other countries were accepting only a few Jewish refugees, if any. Because of connections Mr. Hahn had established while doing business in the United States, Cornelia's family did not need a quota number. As they bypassed the line, one man held up his child – a boy dressed in a tweed coat with a brown velvet collar and brown buttons. "Can't somebody help us?" the man cried.

Such a confusing mix of emotions Cornelia felt. Shame – she had done nothing to earn the privilege of bypassing the line. Gratitude – yet, if not for their good fortune . . . Compassion and desperation – if she could, she would help all the people in line, but what could one teenaged girl do? What could *anyone* do? The image of that line and that boy would stay with Cornelia for the rest of her life.

On November 23, 1938, as the Hahns were finishing their chocolate bread pudding, the phone rang. It was time to leave. Cornelia's mother handed her a silver mesh purse. "Go quickly, Nele, and bury this in the forest behind the house."

Cornelia ran, dug a hole in the earth under a tree, and buried it.

Back at the house, her mother asked, "Where is the purse?"

"I buried it," Cornelia said.

"The whole purse? I meant for you to bury only the coins."

Her stomach churning – how stupid she had been – Cornelia asked, "Shall I go and dig it up?"

"Never mind," her mother said. "We must go now."

Taking with them one small suitcase each, Cornelia, Charlotte, and their mother left their home to pick up Sir Alexander Lawrence at his hotel. A friend of Cornelia's Uncle Kurt and a lawyer in Great Britain, he had agreed to travel with them to England. The plan was to go by train from the Bahnhof Zoo railway station to Aix-la-Chapelle near the border of Belgium and the Netherlands. From there, they would make their way to England, and eventually travel by ship to the United States.

On the way to the station, they stopped at the American Consulate to collect their passports. They also took time to say goodbye to Cornelia's beloved grandmother. She refused to join them on their journey because she didn't believe it was right to leave the country of one's forefathers.

Under strict instructions to be quiet no matter what happened, Cornelia boarded the train. With all the determination of a stubborn seventeen year old, she decided she would look only forward from that moment on.

As the train pulled out of the station, she did not look back. Soon it passed the shell of a building burned out by the Nazis. Cornelia's younger sister asked, "Who set fire to that building?" Mrs. Hahn shushed her and glanced around uneasily.

At the border, Nazis boarded the train. One of the men yelled, "Mrs. Hahn, get out!" Cornelia's heart leapt into her throat.

Alexander Lawrence stood up. "I'm accompanying this lady," he said. "Why should she get out?" He then engaged the Nazi officer in a polite conversation about having recently attended a conference and being impressed by the lawfulness of Germany society. He managed to keep the officer talking until the train began pulling out of the station. As it did, the Nazi officer jumped off.

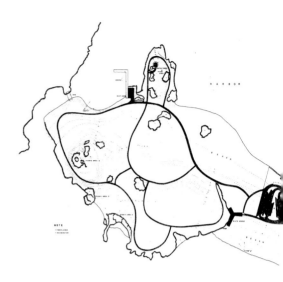

Chapter Four

New Roots

Cornelia's student assignment above shows a sketch for a park by a harbor. It includes planning for traffic routes, picnic areas, parking, and assorted buildings.

On February 23, 1939, Cornelia landed in New York aboard the *Queen Mary*, wanting nothing more than to blend into the American scene. She wanted saddle shoes, white socks, and short hair like everyone else. "Please," she begged her mother, "please won't you cut off my braids?"

Cornelia's mother worked hard so her daughters could go to college. She bought a farm in New Hampshire. Every morning, to get her "firecracker" of a daughter out of her way, Mrs. Hahn sent Cornelia to the nearby town market with the vegetables they'd grown. Loading their station wagon with the harvest, she could hardly wait to get on with fulfilling her dream of becoming a landscape architect.

What was this profession that Cornelia was so intent on pursuing? Many people think of it as "making gardens" or even "planting shrubs and flowers," but it's much more than that.

It's designing spaces in the out of doors. Whether for a small garden or a city park, it involves planning how those spaces will look and how people will use them. Where should the building sit? What can be done to ensure public safety and access for those with disabilities? By what route will people get from one area of a site to another? How can problems like reducing vandalism around a school or erosion of a riverbank be solved?

16

A landscape architect's work is similar to that of a landscape painter, except that the landscape architect uses natural materials – earth, rock, water, and plants – instead of paints, and possibly structures like fences and gazebos as well.

A year after arriving in the States, Cornelia was keen to go to Smith College in Northampton, Massachusetts. The school offered an interdepartmental major in Architecture and Landscape Architecture and many of the professors there also taught at Harvard. Smith was reluctant to admit her – supposedly because of her accent. Cornelia suspected it was because she was Jewish. Whatever the reason, when she showed them her 96 percent average from high school, they let her in.

As she made her way up the long driveway, Cornelia was struck by the majestic oaks and London plane trees on campus. The beautiful botanical garden and arboretum (a living museum of woody plants) added to the thrill of learning about plant materials, construction, the history of landscape architecture and architecture drawing, and about how much fun it was to conduct research with actual plant materials instead of through books.

But it was a somber time at Smith College, too. Many friends and the brothers of friends were being drafted into the army. One day, someone came to Cornelia with the *New York Times* and pressed her to read it. She didn't want to face the ugliness in stories and pictures about the war and concentration camps. She wanted to focus all her attention on her studies.

During field trips to analyze various sites, Cornelia never complained about cold feet, sweltering heat, or muscles that ached from lugging survey equipment and other paraphernalia around town. She was too excited about tackling design problems to notice. She also loved hearing professors later analyze the strengths and weaknesses in how different students solved the challenges each site presented – poor drainage, perhaps, high winds, or the need to make a park that everyone, from soccer players to senior citizens, could enjoy.

Over the years at Smith College Cornelia learned "3 P's" that would stand her in good stead as a landscape architect and would have been useful no matter what profession she had chosen:

This student project is a perspective drawing of a house to be built on a steep site at the edge of the sea.

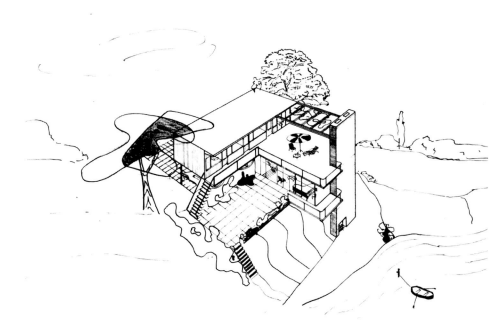

1. Be **Patient**. People often need time to come round to your way of thinking.

2. Be **Persistent**. Stand up for what you know is right.

3. Be **Polite**. People are more likely to be convinced by your arguments if you present them in a pleasant manner.

One of the most exciting discoveries Cornelia made at Smith College was the work of Frederick Law Olmsted, considered by many to be "the father of landscape architecture." In the late 1880s, he had designed Central Park in New York City and Mount Royal Park in Montreal. He had also designed the Smith College campus, the work there taking him into the early twentieth century. His aim was not to *conquer* nature (as many gardeners in the past tried to do), but to work *with* nature. One way to do this was to use plants that grow naturally in an area, and therefore need little care. Olmsted understood that it can take years – generations even – for a designer to see the fruits of his labors. He believed that creating open public spaces for *everyone* to enjoy was

18

When Frederick Law Olmsted founded the American Society of Landscape Architects in 1899, he used the term "landscape architect" to help make it clear that what its members did – they *designed* – was different from gardening. He knew the struggle to make a distinction between gardening and landscape architecture would continue beyond his lifetime.

And it has. Time and again, Cornelia has had to tell people, "I am not a gardener." Like other landscape architects, she is interested in plants, trees, turf, water, rocks, and bridges primarily as elements of "the painting" she is composing. For example, to her roses are flecks of white or red that can be used to modify a mass of green, or a way of introducing a pleasant scent to a sitting area.

Kathy Stinson

of utmost importance. All these ideas felt "right" to Cornelia, and fed the fires of her passion to fulfill her childhood dream.

But not *every* class thrilled her. She found it especially hard to rouse herself for an early morning botany class – not because it was early, but because the professor's methods left no room to be creative. One morning she had to throw her clothes on over her pajamas to avoid being late. Another time she arrived at school hungry and helped herself to a plateful of fruit. The professor sternly informed her that the fruits were to have been studied during that morning's class for the different kinds of seeds they held. (Cornelia refrained from informing him that the seeds of the pear, plum, and grapes were, in fact, still intact. The professor suspended her for four weeks anyway, and Cornelia had to learn what she missed from classmates in order to pass the course.)

chapter five

New Buds

Before computers became the tool of choice for many landscape architects, tools like these were used for laying out designs and labeling them.

The early years of the twentieth century were tough for women interested in landscape architecture. In 1898, one young woman's parents told her that her decision to study landscape architecture would bring dishonor to the whole family. She walked around the block three times before bringing herself to climb the steps at the Massachusetts Institute of Technology.

At least MIT accepted female students. One of the best schools for aspiring landscape architects, the Harvard School of Design, was open only to men. When the school refused admission to a determined young woman in 1915, Professor Henry Frost agreed to tutor her in the living room of her home. A year later she and four more women were being taught in the office that Frost shared with his colleague, Bremmer Pond, in Harvard Square. Many men on campus condescendingly referred to the arrangement as "The Frost and Pond Day Nursery."

Once the United States entered World War II in 1941, many young men joined the fight, and Harvard's enrollment figures dropped. The school decided to admit women "for the duration of the war."

For Cornelia Hahn, the timing couldn't have been better. At Harvard she added to what she had learned at Smith – about basic design, surveying a site, ground contours, road construction, elementary drainage, and construction of

20

architectural features such as steps, terraces, pools, and walls.

Among Cornelia's professors at Harvard was Walter Gropius, the head of the Department of Architecture. His famous style of making art involved many people collaborating on a single creation. In a way, it provided a model for a democratic, co-operative society. Given what had happened in Germany under Hitler, it's not hard to understand why Cornelia found Gropius's ideal so attractive.

During her first year at Harvard, Cornelia lived with an aunt and made breakfast for the family before riding off to school on her bicycle each day. One morning she arrived to see a young man stepping out of a very posh car. His name was Pierre Elliott Trudeau. Of course, no one knew then that he would one day (in 1968) become prime minister of Canada, or that the young woman carefully balancing her papers and drawing equipment in the basket of her bicycle would one day (in 1990) be awarded a prestigious Order of Canada – the first landscape architect to be so honored.

Kathy Stinson

At a picnic at Walden Pond in 1945, a Harvard student took a second bite of cake studded with raisins and asked, "Who brought this wonderful cake?"

Someone nodded toward the young woman chatting with classmates under a tree, its leaves drifting to the yellow circle beneath it. "Cornelia Hahn."

The young man strolled over to compliment her on her cake.

"I didn't make it," she said off-handedly. "My aunt did."

The young man, whose name was Peter, said, "I have not seen *gugelhupf* since I left Vienna."

Cornelia guessed he had likely left Austria when the Nazis invaded, but it was a lovely day at Walden Pond, Europe was far away, and she didn't ask. They chatted only about the picnic and their courses and skipped stones across the water. (Peter was doing his Master's degree in city and regional planning, having earned his Bachelor's degree in city planning at McGill University in Montreal.) Gathering picnic baskets and folding blankets,

21

Cornelia and Peter spent happy times at the beach near her mother's farm in New Hampshire. This photo was taken a few months after their 1953 marriage.

Cornelia hoped she would see Peter again.

Months passed and he didn't call. Finally in March he did. He said he was sorry it had taken him so long, but he'd been studying from morning to night with a German guest of Professor Gropius – the director of city planning from Berlin. Cornelia didn't know whether to be annoyed or impressed.

"Would you like to go see a movie with me?" Peter asked.

"What's showing?"

"*You Can't Take It With You*." It was a movie Cornelia was dying to see.

At 6:30, as promised, Peter arrived at the door of the apartment where

Cornelia was living with a friend. He was carrying a T-square, a drawing board, and a satchel. "I'm working on a management study for a new town," he said. "If you'll help me for two hours, we can still make the late show."

The study was to include streets, buildings, vegetation, lights, curbs – everything the new town would need. As Cornelia and Peter worked on the assignment, they forgot all about their movie. Late that night, they chased each other around the apartment, snapping twisted towels, and waking Cornelia's snoring roommate. Then they went back to work.

Kathy Stinson

After working together for forty-eight hours, Cornelia knew that Peter Oberlander was the man she would marry – some day.

🍃

When Cornelia graduated with her Bachelor of Landscape Architecture degree in 1947, Professor Bremmer Pond (of the former "Frost and Pond Day Nursery") gave her a letter of recommendation, describing her as "a person of imagination, efficient, and capable." In a more personal letter, he told her he had enjoyed teaching her "despite her foibles." It seems Cornelia was a woman of attitude even then.

> What we now call landscape architecture was originally practiced by gardeners, horticulturalists, civil engineers, and occasionally architects. The first documented use of the term "landscape architecture" occurred in 1840 when John Claudius London published *The landscape gardening and landscape architecture of the late Humphrey Repton, esq. being his entire works on these subjects*. (Yes, it was as stuffy and male a profession back then as it sounds!)

chapter six

A Flower Opens

To establish herself in her career, Cornelia went to work for the Citizen's Council for Planning in Philadelphia and then for New York's Regional Plan Association. Meanwhile, Peter went to work briefly in London, England, and then in Ottawa.

One day, after meeting with a community group about a playground, Cornelia was coming out of a drugstore. The pavement was hot and children were hanging around with nothing to do. Cornelia thought, 'It's too bad these kids don't have the chance to enjoy nature the way I did.' Across the street from the drugstore was an empty lot. The earth was cracked and dry with a few dusty weeds poking through it. 'But this *could* be a wonderful place for mothers and children.'

Most people saw only an empty lot as they passed by – if they noticed it at all. Cornelia was seeing possibilities. Green grass for children to run and roll in. Trees for them to climb. Benches for mothers to sit on. She went to city hall to find out who owned the property, and talked them into letting her design a park there.

An architect, impressed with that work and her imagination, hired her to help design an entire housing project, and that job led to another. Here she was, at thirty, doing at last what she'd dreamed of since she was eleven years old! It was invigorating work – making the grounds of large, impersonal, public housing projects more inviting. In September 1954, a project Cornelia was involved with

Notice how even in Cornelia's early designs, she liked to use lots of one kind of plant – like the fescue grasses and heathers in the garden on the facing page. Above is an area she designed at the Faculty Club at the University of British Columbia.

25

It takes a well-trained artistic mind to be able to look at an area – an industrial block, a building site, or a soggy vacant field – and see possibilities there for parkland, a new housing project, or a series of gardens. But it also takes technical know-how to figure out how to make a possibility a reality. Landscape architects can get pretty excited about things like "grading" – making the land flat or sloped and by how much and in which direction – and "drainage." *Drainage? Who can get excited about where rainwater goes?* A landscape architect does, and you do too, if someone hasn't planned carefully to make sure it doesn't flood your basement – or your whole neighborhood.

was written up in *Life* magazine – a big deal for a landscape architect in the early days of her career, and terrific encouragement to continue.

But work wasn't her only love. Cornelia's sights were still firmly fixed on the man she'd met at the picnic at the magical Walden Pond. He had accepted a position at the School of Architecture at the University of British Columbia in Vancouver and he wanted to know: would she go there with him?

It would mean saying goodbye to the culture of the East that she so loved – the theaters, the museums, the *life!* But, in the West, she would have the opportunity to conquer new ground. Oh, but the Rocky Mountains were so oppressive! Could she "make friends with them" in time? Compared to other cities she'd lived in, Vancouver seemed like a small town.

Yes, and to go there would make her feel like a pioneer! Besides, she loved Peter, he loved her, and they had been apart for long enough. On January 2, 1953, they were married at New York's city hall. Soon after, they pulled up in front of a white clapboard house near the University of British Columbia.

Peter politely opened the door to their illegal flat on the third floor and said. "Cornelia, I have to go to a meeting. There's a grocery store just down the street."

If Cornelia felt sorry for herself, as many young wives might have, it wasn't for long. She had her own work to do, collaborating on the design of a house and garden for someone Peter had met through his work at the university.

chapter seven

Spaces for Playing

S oon Cornelia and Peter moved into a house of their own, built on stilts in a large meadow. Their first child, Judith Antonia Eleanor, was born in 1956, followed by Timothy Frederick Albert in 1958, and Wendy Elizabeth Rose in 1960.

Cornelia offered Judy, Tim, and Wendy lots of activities – playing at sports, painting, music lessons, reading books. She believed, "Give them every range of possibility and they will bite."

During the years Cornelia was raising her children, she didn't practice landscape architecture full-time. Children were not young for long, and there'd be plenty of time for her career later. Like many mothers, Cornelia spent hours perched on the edge of a sandbox while her children played. As she watched them making castles and mud pies, it struck her that children seemed to have a real need to create things – and wasn't it great that a simple sand pile could help satisfy it?

Watching Tim build sand castles inspired Cornelia to use earthen mounds in more of her landscape designs. Also called "berms," mounds are really just giant sand castles. But they are also a good way to screen out traffic noise and to save money by providing a place to bury scrap building materials or rubble left over from a demolished structure.

Like her mother before her, young Wendy Oberlander loved climbing trees.

Mounds also allowed for what Cornelia felt was one of the most important elements in any landscape – surprise. A mound forced you either to go around it, or over it, and when you did, you discovered something new – a different view, a statue, a track to follow into a thicket of shrubs, a pond to float sticks in, or perhaps a new friend to play with. Way more interesting to discover such things than to see them all at once when you entered a park or garden.

After creating several gardens for homeowners and at the University of British Columbia Faculty Club, Cornelia was hired to design a public playground. Given where she was spending good parts of each day, it was an appropriate assignment.

One day, pushing Wendy higher and higher on the swing, she thought about an interesting play space she had read about in Copenhagen, Denmark. The Junk Playground was devised by a landscape architect named Sorenson in 1943. He had noticed that kids often chose to mess around in junkyards and building sites, instead of in the beautiful playgrounds he had designed for them. In an area of Copenhagen where juvenile delinquency was a problem, Sorenson set up a four-acre (1.6-hectare) "park" where construction workers were invited to dump unused building materials. Kids of all ages came and built things. They lost interest in the structures once they were built, so the city sent someone each October to tear them down. The kids could then take the raw materials and start again to create something new.

Such a contrast to playgrounds Cornelia had seen in Vancouver and other cities – level areas of asphalt with a swing set and teeter-totter bolted down in the middle. How were children supposed to use their imaginations in a place like that?! Why not design a playground that provided scrap materials for building things, a playground with hills and tunnels, and a tree house?

Another day, as Tim scrambled into the ravine after Judy and they began damming the stream at the bottom with sticks and stones, Cornelia thought, 'All children should have woods and water to play in.' Then, 'Why not incorporate into city playgrounds the kind of "natural" places to play that her children enjoyed, and which she had loved too? After all, if kids don't have contact with nature, how will they ever come to understand it, learn to care about it, respect

Cornelia and her family enjoy time outdoors at a cabin near their home in Vancouver in 1967. No matter how busy she was professionally, Cornelia always found a way to make time for Peter and her children.

29

The first playground, as we think of it, was the *kindergarten* created in Germany in1840 by Friederich Froebel, who believed that play is an effective educational activity. Most people at that time thought his idea was nonsense, but according to Froebel, "Play is never nonsense." In a book called *The Training of the Human Plant*, botanist Luther Burbank wrote, "The wonders of nature should be a daily part of children's lives."

it, and cooperate with it? If kids are to grow up and be caretakers rather than destroyers of life on our beautiful blue Earth, there *has* to be a way to make contact with nature possible!'

During the 1950s, Cornelia become a specialist in children's playgrounds, and wherever there was a natural feature on a site – a tree to climb, bushes to hide in, a hill to slide down, or a stream for kids to dam or float things in – she preserved it. If there were none of these things on a site, she planted or created them. To encourage creative play, Cornelia's playgrounds included sand deep enough to make castles and available in a way it wouldn't blow out of its container or into children's eyes. There were loose materials like those Sorenson had provided in Copenhagen: wooden boxes of different sizes, boards, small ladders, blocks, loose wood, old tires, lengths of clothes line, "beautiful junk" like wash tubs, old pots and pans. And there were playhouses, tarpaulins, old blankets, and caves or nooks.

Limited budgets sometimes meant Cornelia couldn't do everything she hoped to, but she loved knowing that in designing her playgrounds, she was providing neighborhoods – first in Philadelphia and then in Vancouver – with something truly valuable. And in truth, she was having as much fun planning the playgrounds as kids had playing in them.

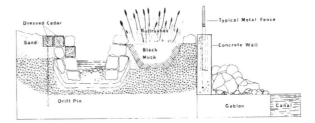

Dressed Cedar
Bullrushes
Typical Metal Fence
Sand
Black Muck
Concrete Wall
Drift Pin
Gabion
Canal

chapter eight

A Playground for 30,000 Children

I n 1967, Canada pulled out all the stops for its centennial year with its first world's fair. That same year *O Canada* became the country's national anthem and Canadian hockey player Curtis Joseph was born. 1967 was the year the Beatles released one of rock's most proclaimed record albums, *Sgt. Pepper's Lonely Hearts Club Band*, the world saw its first electronic cash machine – in England – and American actress Julia Roberts was born.

The federal government decided that the Canada Pavilion at Expo 67 should include a Children's Creative Centre and hired Cornelia to design it. The outdoor play area she was given to work with was no larger than most city lots, because organizers hoped visitors to the fair would be inspired to build similar facilities in their own communities.

Cornelia knew that, like her other playgrounds, the Expo 67 playground must provide lots of opportunity for kids to do the things they loved: run, climb, crawl, build, dig, and get wet. So, she planned for sand areas, shade trees, logs large enough to build life-size structures, and a covered area for artistic play. There would of course be a mound, and a canal, too. In the canal would sit a recycled Nova Scotia dory, chained in place to keep it from tipping over. Children could sit inside it, rock it, and pretend to row.

Not everyone was thrilled with Cornelia's ideas. Some who saw her

Both artistic vision and technical know-how are behind design drawings like the one above for a section of the Expo 67 playground.

31

design fretted about safety. What if a child hit someone with a log or dropped one on someone's foot? Wouldn't kids wreck things that weren't bolted down? Wouldn't they get slivers?

Cornelia insisted that the features she had designed were important, that children need the dramatic and creative play situations these features would provide. "Many people are so paralyzed by worst-case scenarios that they ignore the tremendous *positive* potential of children. Let them learn the feeling of being the ones to start something in a play situation, and they will achieve true self-expression and self-fulfillment. Let them find out what it is to be truly involved in play with other children and with materials that invite them to use their imaginations, and they will grow up to be involved citizens with the imagination to solve problems in their own lives and in their communities."

The day she watched a small girl play at the water's edge for an hour, even though it was cold out, and other children cooperating on building a house together, even though they didn't know each other, Cornelia knew she had been right to be persistent. When one Expo visitor was overheard saying, "A playground without swings and slides? Why, it's simply . . . *un-Canadian!*" she simply shook her head.

It had taken about 700 hours to design the playground at Expo 67. What took the most time was not coming up with ideas, but the highly skilled technical work of producing specifications and detailed drawings for every aspect of construction. In a business sense, Cornelia didn't earn enough for the job to justify the hours she had spent on it, but the results were so satisfying she didn't care.

People from more than sixty countries had come to Expo and observed how children loved to climb into the tree house, slide down the pole to the ground, how they engaged in imaginative play inside it and all around it for hours on end. They saw children damming the stream, drawing on the outdoor chalkboard, building things with logs, bouncing in the commando net, and creating works of art by winding different colors and textures of wool around pegs sticking out of a wall. There weren't many children using the hollow log intended as a quiet space away from the hubbub of the fair for those feeling overwhelmed by it. Hot and tired children seemed to prefer playing quietly with construction toys, probably because there was more they could do with them.

The Report to the Commissioner General of the Canadian Pavilion at Expo noted that "the excellent arrangements of mounds and flat spaces, sand, water, and covered areas," was an important factor in how well the children played. And, "When one piece of equipment was in great demand," the report said, "children quickly went to something else, due to the ingenious arrangement. Even at peak periods, with 150 children in a space 60' x 120', it did not seem overcrowded."

Kathy Stinson

During the six months of the fair, not one child fell from the tree house or got more than a "soaker" in the canal. In fact, the only injury reported was a sprained ankle. Not bad, given that 30,000 children had played there!

Other playground planners were excited about the new, imaginative ideas they saw. They also were impressed that the cost of building such a playground was barely half what an ordinary playground cost.

After Expo 67, similar playgrounds sprang up all over North America – and beyond – inspired by the one on which Cornelia had lavished so much time, thought, and passion.

The wooden dory in the canal in the Expo 67 playground Cornelia designed was chained in place, but children loved to climb in and pretend to row.

chapter nine

Her Own Garden

Standing on a street not far from the University of British Columbia, Cornelia surveyed the wide lot at the edge of a ravine full of hemlock, cedar, oregon maple, and the sounds of birds. This was where she and Peter would build their second house and garden. What fun it would be to apply their professional know-how to their own place! (Completed in 1970, it would still be their home in 2008.)

They had already decided where on the lot the house, designed by Peter, with Cornelia's input, would sit. Cornelia's landscape design – with Peter's input – would aim to make it seem inevitable that the house should be where they put it.

In making her plans, Cornelia had to first "read" the site.

Begin by considering the lay of the land and water. She remembered the advice of the Japanese noble that had so impressed her grandmother. Cornelia squeezed a handful of soil to get a sense of the plants that would grow well on their property without a lot of care. Checking its depth here and there around the site, she discovered a large mass of bedrock. Water would, of course, drain right off it, and into the ravine.

Study the work of past masters. From Olmsted's work, Cornelia had learned much about preserving natural scenery, and using native plants – plants that

35

grow in an area even when they aren't planted there – and how much freer a garden feels when it isn't entirely clear where it ends.

Recall the places of beauty that you know. First to spring to mind were the gardens she had played in as a child. In their open spaces she'd felt free and expansive. Their more secluded areas felt secret and safe.

So, how would she give their new garden a sense of both privacy and space?

First a mound – to help block the view of the street, muffle traffic noise, create an intimate area outside their home, and give privacy to those inside. Then plant the mound with a hemlock hedge and pine trees. Under the trees, plant shade-loving rhododendrons, azaleas, mosses, ferns, periwinkle, and lily of the valley. For a totally different texture, add some clumps of wild grasses. Clearly, the wooded ravine would not be changed – except for a couple of rhododendrons she would plant close to the house.

Then, on your chosen site, let memory speak, and make into your own that which moves you most. Imagining how she, Peter, and their visitors would approach their property, how they would enter the house, where they might grow vegetables, and where their children would play, Cornelia roughed out many possible layouts. She turned her drawings upside down and sideways so she could imagine what she would see,

Even during a Vancouver January, the garden at the Oberlanders' home is a lush oasis of calm

hear, and smell walking through the garden from different directions.

Cornelia and Peter agreed that they didn't want to use herbicides or chemical fertilizers on their property, so a traditional, grassy lawn was out of the question, especially in a shady yard like theirs.

"It would be an invitation to years of frustration."

"And who has time for all that watering and mowing anyway?"

". . . How about a lawn of moss instead?" Moss was native to the area so it would grow pretty much by itself, and would look like a beautiful green rug.

For a few splashes of color, they'd plant flowers in pots around the yard. And they'd create a vegetable garden in the sunny area up a slope and off to one side of the house.

Before designing a final plan that balanced the limits of climate, sunlight, soil type, future needs of her husband and family, and the budget they had to work with, Cornelia consulted with contractors to be sure all her ideas were workable. "The idea of something is grandiose, but the details, they kill you," Cornelia warns. "If you aren't a stickler for the details – like what size holes are best for the bottom of a plant container, or the angle and diameter of a drainage pipe – then your designs don't come to life. I am a stickler!"

Cornelia was also stubborn. Included in her design were several existing trees that city authorities told her must be removed because they were in danger of falling. She said, "Nonsense," and refused to take them down. More than thirty five years later, they still stand, sheltering a secluded wild garden.

While Cornelia's home and garden were being built, she continued designing gardens and more playgrounds for clients. She had built seventy or so playgrounds when her aunt finally sat her down one day to say, "Cornelia, you've done enough playgrounds. This just can't go on. You should do bigger things."

At that moment, the phone rang.

"This is Bing Thom calling from Arthur Erickson's office."

Cornelia gripped the receiver tightly. Arthur Erickson was *the guru* of architecture in Canada. "Bigger things" were about to happen.

Kathy Stinson

chapter ten

Nature in the City

Erickson and the architects in his office were, in 1974, working on plans for Robson Square. Bing Thom described the Robson Square project, then said, "Cornelia, can you report to us tomorrow morning with your ideas about plants that would suit the site, and how you would go about bringing nature into the city?"

Much as she loved designing playgrounds, Cornelia was itching to work on something bigger. She stayed up most of the night to prepare for the next day's meeting.

To the Erickson team of men gathered to hear her proposal Cornelia said, "How to bring nature to this site will depend on a number of technical matters. What will the holding capacity of the roof be?" (In other words, how much weight could it hold?) "What can be done about waterproofing to ensure that the roof doesn't leak? How can it be protected against roots that might try to grow through it? What will the plants grow in (soil being too heavy), and how deep must it be to allow for the planting of trees? What systems will be put in place for irrigating and fertilizing the plants and for drainage? What kind of budget will there be for the installation and maintenance of the landscaping?"

Erickson had approached Cornelia because of her strong background in horticulture, but clearly, this woman knew a lot more than just plants! Before

Robson Square occupies three city blocks in downtown Vancouver. The law courts, the provincial government building, and the art gallery are all linked by a series of public open spaces, on rooftops.

39

lunchtime that day, he asked Cornelia to join his team.

Seeing the project as an apprenticeship, Cornelia devoted herself to studying things like slope restoration, pavement, and city bylaws for safety requirements. For each of the seven areas of the site she drew up a large chart with the headings Water, Plant Material, Pavement Treatment, Wall Treatment, Furniture, Sound, Smell, and Activities. Some headings were subdivided. Sound, for example, had room for "Existing" (mostly related to traffic) and "Possible Additional" (through the use of wind chimes and waterfalls).

Research led Cornelia to the discovery of a lightweight growing medium that was a mix of peat, sand, and perlite. She knew that it would provide adequate nourishment and support for trees without overburdening the roof, but the project architects and engineers were skeptical. It took her three years and hauling bags of various unsuitable alternatives into their offices to convince them she was right, and to keep her vision of trees on the roof alive.

Cornelia had always liked the dramatic effect of planting many of one kind of plant, as opposed to a few of this and a few of that – a style of gardening she once compared (although she hates to admit it) to making pizza. She has also said, "Mixing a whole bunch of plants is like wearing five different polka-dot dresses at the same time." At one point in the development of plans for Robson Square, she proposed planting one area all in yews. "But, Cornelia," Arthur Erickson gently pointed out, "there are many greens." She changed her plan to include laurels with dark shiny leaves and memorial roses with lighter, chartreuse leaves. The result was a wonderfully rich tapestry of greens.

When the work was all done, people could cross the three city blocks of Robson Square in endless ways – diagonally, up, down, or across – all safely away from street traffic. Slopes and stramps (a clever combination of stairs and ramps designed by the architects) led pedestrians over rooftops at different levels without their even being aware of it. Cornelia's favorite spot was a peaceful area set apart by mounds (made of Styrofoam) planted with pines, Japanese maples, and white azaleas. She loved how the blossoms seemed almost to glow, especially in shadow.

Robson Square has been called "a magnificent oasis in the middle of

Vancouver." Among its concrete and glass forms were planted some 50,000 plants – pines, magnolias, rhododendrons, azaleas, vines, roses, dogwoods, and forty citrus trees salvaged from an orchard in California. There were plants everywhere – outside, inside, under glass, among steps, ramps, and fountains, and cascading down walls. When you were in its gardens, with their towering trees and cool, shady corners, it was – and still is – hard to believe you were on a roof in the center of a major city.

The landscaping at Robson Square provided places of sunshine and shadow, large gathering areas, semi-private walkways, and quiet resting places.

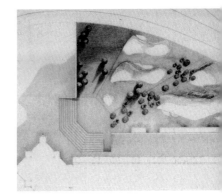

chapter eleven

Trees Majestic, Ugly, and Old

On one side of Robson Square, along Hornby Street, Cornelia planted a double row of Red Sunset maples. By providing shade in summer, color in the fall, "and even the gray bark in winter is pleasant," she says, they extend the sense of being in a park right out to the curb. City engineers wanted the trees to be set thirty feet (9 m) apart, but Cornelia and Arthur Erickson argued that to give people on the sidewalk a feeling of being protected from the street, the rain, and the sun, the trees must be only fifteen feet (4.5 m) apart.

Had Cornelia not exercised her 3 P's, Patience, Persistence, and Politeness, the lovely effect along Hornby would not have been created. Her plans included an underground system that ensured easy watering and fertilizing, especially important for trees surrounded by concrete.

Of all the plant materials a landscape architect has to play with, trees have always been Cornelia's favorites. Why? They make us feel good! *Trees in the City*, a book that Cornelia and Ira Nadel, an English professor at UBC, co-authored in 1977, explains how. To summarize:

Trees shield people from sun and rain, and cool down hot humid air. They provide a brilliant contrast to a drab world of concrete. The hard, straight lines of curbs, streets and buildings, make people feel

Circles like those on the plan above translate into gorgeous trees once the plan is implemented. A landscape architect can envision how those trees will look from every angle that people will come upon them, and how much space they will take up when fully grown. The existing Douglas firs (opposite) were preserved on the site of the C.K. Choi Institute at UBC.

43

restless. Trees break up those lines. Trees trap pollutants like sulfur dioxide, peroxyacetyl nitrate, and ozone. They reduce the intensity of wind in wind tunnels and muffle unpleasant noise. (Studies show that people feel crabbier in noisy places.) And like most plants, trees remove carbon dioxide from the air and give off oxygen. (It takes eighteen trees to produce the oxygen one person needs to breathe.)

Have you ever felt, not only good, but a sense of wonder or even *awe*, when surrounded by trees? According to Cornelia, "Trees are a tenuous connection between our longing for paradise and the harsh reality of the landscapes of our paved-over cities. They are the link between earth and sky. They reach up to the stars, the moon, and the sun, yet are anchored firmly in the ground and have held hands with Architecture from ancient times onward."

As each of the Oberlander children was born, Cornelia and Peter planted an apple tree in their garden. Cornelia says, "A tree represents the continuity of history and permanence, for they require generations to grow up and grow old."

The ancient Babylonians and Persians considered trees to be sacred objects. The ancient Egyptians carried trees 1,500 miles (2,400 km) by boat to transplant them.

When deciding which trees to plant in a land-scape, Cornelia considers the size and shape a tree will be when fully grown and where it will be placed. Close to a street? Near a building? In an open park? She considers the texture of its bark, the shape of its branches, the smell of its blossoms in spring, and the color of its leaves in fall. Also important are the climate of the place, how fast the tree will grow, its resistance to disease, and how easy it will be to take care of. And of course, as with any element of her design, how the trees will look from every angle that a person might come upon them.

Have you ever noticed how some trees look dignified – majestic even – while others look like someone just plunked them down somewhere? Cornelia hates to see a tree squashed against a building (because someone didn't plan for its growth) or in a space that looks "left over" once all the other work on a site has been done. Finding a proper place for a tree right at the start of planning a landscape design, she believes, is a crucial part of reflecting its dignity and value. "Being treated as an afterthought," she says, "is degrading to any living being."

"She's crazy!" said a member of the all-male board of directors after hearing Cornelia's design proposal for the National Gallery of Canada site in Ottawa. Another man, tried hard to remain calm as he reasoned with her, "Cornelia, no one uses jack pines in an urban setting. Their wood is weak, and they aren't . . . pretty."

A third man agreed. "It's Austrian pine that the site wants. Much nicer."

Cornelia responded, "But haven't we agreed that this area should reflect the landscapes visitors will see in the Group of Seven paintings inside the gallery? Aren't we trying to replicate a rocky northern taiga?"

There were quiet mumblings of agreement, but Cornelia knew that at least one man at the table was thinking, 'Forty people interviewed for this job and they had to hire this one?!'

Cornelia held up a photo of an A.Y. Jackson painting. "Look. The trees in this painting are gnarly and bent. They grow in a harsh climate and in very little soil. And that's what is needed here."

Another board member sighed. "Be reasonable, Cornelia. Who wants to look at a bunch of bent-over trees?"

"Better they should look at so many pretty little Christmas trees?" she retorted.

Cornelia eventually bowed to the committee's overwhelming wish for Austrian pines, but left the meeting determined to search out the most "Charlie Brown" of Christmas trees available at the nursery. When the shipment of stunted, irregularly shaped trees arrived, she donned hard hat and construction boots and grabbed a shovel. She wanted to be sure the trees would be planted at the proper angle so they would grow into even more irregular shapes – like the wind-swept trees in the Group of Seven paintings.

Other areas of the grounds around Ottawa's National Gallery mimicked other styles of artwork hanging there. The project was completed in 1988. The next year, the Canadian Society of Landscape Architects recognized the brilliance behind the landscaping and awarded Cornelia its highest honor – the National Award of Excellence. Of her work on the gallery, Cornelia said, "At its best, landscape architecture creates a dialogue between art and nature, taking inspiration from both."

At the site of the C.K. Choi Institute for Asian Studies at the University of British Columbia, Cornelia insisted (in 1993) on preserving an existing stand of eighty-year-old Douglas firs, with selected lower limbs removed to let more light into the building. People in the building have said they feel as if they're working in a forest – exactly what Cornelia intended. (More on this environmentally responsible building and landscaping in Chapter Thirteen.)

On the same project, she planted a row of ginkgo trees along the street, to absorb pollution and because they're beautiful. One of the oldest known species of trees, ginkgo (also known as the maidenhair tree) has been around for 250 million years. Destroyed during the Ice Age in most regions of Europe and North America, they survived in certain regions of China. They might be extinct today if Buddhist monks had not, for centuries, planted them around their temples.

It is a very durable tree. After the atomic bomb was dropped on Hiroshima in 1945, several ginkgos around the epicenter of the blast survived and re-sprouted without any visible genetic deformation. They are still growing in Hiroshima today and are considered "bearers of hope."

Cornelia became so fascinated with the ginkgo tree on a trip to China that she decided to use its leaf on her business card. It has also been used to decorate the chapter headings of this book.

chapter twelve

Expanding Horizons

The men on the National Capital Commission who had doubted Cornelia's choices and abilities were not alone. There were others – architects, engineers, other landscape architects, and especially older men with more traditional views – who believed she was landing jobs because of her husband's connections at the university. After all, how could a *woman* understand the *technical* aspects of *their* work?

In the 1950s, 80 to 90 percent of landscape architects were men. "Landscape architecture is still a male profession, I hate to tell you," Cornelia once said. "But I never asked what it felt like to cope with obvious biases, because all I could think of was going out there and making the world a little greener. I never looked right or left . . . That's the only way I could succeed in this man's world." (There are more women practicing the profession now, but the number of men is still around 60 to 75 percent.)

When not busy designing landscapes – or hiking or skiing or swimming or being a wife and mother (and later a grandmother) – Cornelia loved to read, both fiction and non-fiction. Some of what she read affected the work she was doing.

In Aldo Leopold's *A Sand County Almanac* (1949) she read, "We abuse the land because we regard it as a commodity belonging to us. When we see the

You might think that by now Cornelia would know all she needs to know to do her work, but she believes strongly that learning is a lifelong process. She has dozens of professional books in her home studio.

47

land as a community to which we belong, we may begin to use it with love and respect." Reading Rachel Carson's *Silent Spring* (1963) made Cornelia even more aware of how people and the land are interconnected, and of the dangers of pesticides. Ian McHarg's *Design with Nature* (1969) gave factual, scientific backbone to her heartfelt reactions to nature's beauty. McHarg quoted Loren Eiseley, a scientist and philosopher, who said:

> Man in space is enabled to look upon the distant earth, a celestial orb, a revolving sphere. He sees it to be green, from the verdure on the land, algae greening the oceans, a green celestial fruit. Looking closely at the earth he perceives blotches, black, brown, gray and from these extend dynamic tentacles upon the green epidermis. These blemishes he recognizes as the cities and works of man and asks, "Is man but a planetary disease?"

McHarg went on to explain how "Nature is a single interactive system and changes to any part will affect the operation of the whole." (His book is still recommended reading in university Landscape Architecture programs.)

All this reading set Cornelia to thinking about how her choices as a landscape architect had an impact on the ecology of the spaces she was designing.

In 1972 Peter Oberlander came home from the first Stockholm conference on the environment so excited about what he'd heard there that Cornelia sat down to read all the papers he had brought back. Of course, she'd heard of pollution (she was by then fifty-one years old), but with increasing alarm she learned more about the thinning of the planet's protective ozone layer and about climate change that scientists knew was happening even then. Cornelia looked up from the Stockholm papers. "Peter," she said, "we must do something about these problems!" That's exactly what he thought, too.

In the 1980s, landscape architect Garrett Eckbo wrote, "Nature is not a passive storehouse of resources from which we may take as we please. It is rather a seamless web from which man is inseparable." What a relief it was to know she wasn't alone in her growing concern about the environment.

Then, in 1987, she read a report that had just come out of an international conference in Norway. The Brundtland Report was named after Norway's prime minister, the country's first female prime minister. Called "Our Common Future" it proposed long-term strategies for achieving "sustainable development." Development must, it said, "meet the needs of the present without compromising the ability of future generations to meet their own needs." In other words, we must not take more from the earth than it can give back. And, the report was saying, it was possible to protect the environment *and* be prosperous economically at the same time.

Kathy Stinson

"Our Common Future" contained ideas Cornelia had believed in for a long time. Now people in the know from twenty-one countries were sharing her view! She came away from reading the report more determined than ever both to practice by its ideals and to speak up more publicly and emphatically for what she believed in.

chapter thirteen

Small Footprints

Cornelia and other members of the design team visit the future site of a new legislative building in Yellowknife, in Canada's arctic.

Closely tied to the idea of sustainable development is Cornelia's philosophy of "least intervention." It means, essentially, "Let's not mess with things here any more than we have to." In 1991, the architects chosen for the new legislative building for Canada's Northwest Territories, Eva Matsuzaki and James Wright (with Gino Pin Architects) wanted a landscape architect on their team who would be sensitive to the natural site – a lakeside setting with a peat bog, outcroppings of rock, and precious stands of small, hundred-year-old spruce trees. Having already worked with Cornelia on projects in various parts of British Columbia, Matsuzaki and Wright knew she was the right person for the job.

It's possible for a landscape architect to be so sensitive to a natural site that ordinary people can hardly tell that any design work has been done. Sometimes this raises the question: Is it design to *not* design? Cornelia would say, "Of course. You have to know when to plan intensely, and when to leave well enough alone. And you have to know the ecology of the site and work with it to heal the land after construction."

As she did with any undertaking, Cornelia started the Yellowknife project by reading the site: its climate, light, the lay of the land, changes in vegetation from season to season and year to year. "Landscape architecture is not a re-invention of

50

the world," she said. "Landscape architecture is growing a piece of what is there. The site must speak. I must find the spirit of the place. What it is that gives the place its character."

In Yellowknife, in Canada's arctic, the average temperature in July is 63 degrees Fahrenheit (17° Celsius). In January it often drops to -22 degrees Fahrenheit (-30° Celsius) and lower. Plenty of plants grow there – kinnikinnick, arctic rose, blueberry, wild cotton, sedges – but they grow slowly. The growing season is short and permafrost a constant condition of the soil. (Almost constant. Climate change is altering this.) It takes a long time for plants to get established – one hundred years for a tree to reach maturity. In 1992, there were no nurseries where you could drop in to pick up replacements for plants that might be damaged by bulldozers.

Cornelia's mission was to preserve the rugged yet delicate beauty of the site. Her plan for replenishing the site after construction? To painstakingly lift and preserve the mats of peat bog that contained cloudberries and other plants hardy enough to thrive in the northern climate, to collect seeds and cuttings from various plants on the site, and then to transport them to Whitehorse and Vancouver, nurture them, and replant them in large quantities

Kathy Stinson

Hardy arctic roses grow in the harsh conditions of Canada's north, where the growing season is very short.

51

once disruption to the site was over.

"Is she crazy?" the locals asked.

Twenty thousand native plants were later returned to the site in Yellowknife and placed in the ground by Cornelia and the contractors. Rather than using topsoil to improve growing conditions, they used a mix of peat and sand from the site. "I have campaigned for many years not to use topsoil because it comes from farmland," says Cornelia, "and when you remove it, you strip the land. We must use the soil that is on the site." The plants around the Legislative Building may have been grown in a mild climate, but because they are genetically true to the harsh climate of the North, they all survived.

Jamie Bastedo, a writer who lives in Yellowknife, would say of the Legislative Building and its setting on a Canadian Broadcasting Corporation Radio North show in February 2005: "I walk around this lake at least once a week and every time I look at this place I just want to get down on my knees or jump in the air or clap my hands. It's just so beautifully integrated with nature – its location, its shape, its colors, the landscaping . . ." He would also tell listeners, "They saved as many trees as possible when they built this place. All trees within eight feet (2.5 m) of the building had to be saved during construction. If any surveyor or contractor broke this rule they were either fined or fired."

🍂

If the National Gallery of Canada project in Ottawa demonstrated a brilliantly creative, artistic mind at work, the C.K. Choi Institute of Asian Studies at UBC in Vancouver revealed Cornelia's keen interest in using science and technology as well as aesthetics to solve environmental problems. She had the unusual chance on this project to be part of a team made up almost entirely of women – and on which women architects, civil engineers, and mechanical engineers held leading positions.

Every decision made by the Choi design team members reflected their wish to minimize the effect human activity would have on the site. The Choi Institute became an example of what the idea "sustainable development" can actually look like.

The building itself sits where there used to be a parking lot, so no green space was lost to what landscape architects call its footprint. Materials for construction were largely salvaged from a nearby building that was being demolished. Sensors automatically dim the lights on a bright day, and even turn them off if a room is vacant. Windows are not sealed, but can be opened and closed according to the temperature outside. The building uses 40 percent less energy than a "normal" structure. This amounts to a saving of $9,600 a year and enough electricity to serve nineteen family homes.

Kathy Stinson

The water systems at Choi show how closely the indoor and outdoor aspects of the design were tied. Since the composting toilets use no water, they don't have to connect to sewers, and their use saves more than 1,500 gallons (6,820 l) of drinkable water per day. That's enough for 3,000 thirsty people. "Imagine how much drinking water could be saved if a whole city were to use composting toilets," Cornelia says. "Not to mention the money to be saved through not having to maintain and expand sewage infrastructures!"

The liquid that flows out of the toilets is called composting tea. Along with the gray water from the basins and sinks (water mixed with soap and stuff washed off dirty dishes), the "tea" flows into a trench that runs along the front of the building. "Sounds disgusting," you say? It's not. The lined trench is filled with gravel and planted with sedges, reeds, and iris. The gravel, the plants' roots, and other microbial life filter the water as it passes through the trench to the far end. Clear and odorless, the water is then used to irrigate the other gardens around the site.

Just a pretty row of plants along the side of a building? Not so! By the time the liquid from composting toilets passes through this trench, it is clean enough to drink — if it weren't being used to irrigate other gardens.

A lot of people think a green building like the Choi Institute must have been far more expensive to construct than a traditional one. In fact, the per-square-foot cost was no more than any other building at UBC. Completed in 1996, it set new standards for environmental responsibility in landscape architecture. The American Institute of Architects included the building in its 2000 Earth Day Top Ten examples of "viable architectural design solutions that protect and enhance the environment."

Meanwhile, green buildings have been designed by others all over the world according to these principles – houses, schools, condominiums, commercial buildings, hospitals, office towers, stores, police stations, libraries, research centers, banks, hotels, a museum, a bakery, and a dog adoption park. If you can build it, you can build it green!

> For a long time the tallest a tree would grow in Yellowknife was 25 to 30 feet (8 to10 m). With average global temperatures rising, arctic trees are starting to grow taller, and northerners are facing problems created by permafrost that no longer stays frozen year-round.

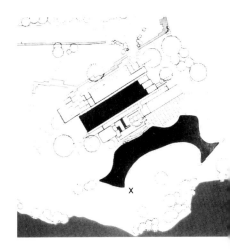

x

The X on the design plan for the Museum of Anthropology marks a spot near the base of a mound from which the photo on page 56 was taken. Lines showing variations in elevation on the original plan are not visible in this reproduction.

chapter fourteen

A Unique Specimen

1. Analyze the site. 2. Collaborate with the design team, the client, and people who will use the site 3. Complete the complex process of creating a design acceptable to everyone, including municipal authorities. 4. Supervise the project as the physical reality of it emerges.

Like most landscape architects, Cornelia followed these steps in all her work. But how she moved through them set her apart from others in her profession.

For one thing, as she began Step 2, she always had a *concept* in mind – an idea that would guide her overall design and the details within it. "Bringing nature into the city" was the concept for Vancouver's Robson Square. Later, knowing how a building would be used often helped her arrive at a concept for its landscaping. The Museum of Anthropology at UBC, for example, was built to showcase the culture of the Haida people, and Cornelia, along with architect Arthur Erickson, decided to simulate a Queen Charlotte Islands Haida community in its outdoor spaces. Since Ottawa's National Gallery of Canada was built to display artwork in various styles, she decided that each outside area should reflect a style of the art hanging inside. The concept for the C.K. Choi Institute from the outset was limiting its footprint.

Arthur Erickson had a different view of what made Cornelia stand out among landscape architects. "One of the most remarkable things about

55

Cornelia is her ability to find a solution to difficult challenges through research," he said. "If I can use her on a project, I do."

Cornelia was so steeped in the habit of research that when Erickson showed her his plans for the new Canadian Chancery in Washington D.C., her immediate response, was "Oh Arthur, that's just like Hadrian's villa! I must read up on Pliny!" (Hadrian was an ancient Roman emperor and Pliny an ancient Roman botanist.) Cornelia found out as much as she could about their elaborate homes and gardens, then planted groundcover azaleas, hanging memorial roses, and hawthorn trees at the level of every balcony, as had been done in ancient Rome.

In her sixty-plus-year career, Cornelia never lost her eagerness to learn all she possibly could about anything that would help her design an outdoor space more effectively. Thanks to "www," as Cornelia refers to the Internet, far more information is more easily available now than it was in the days

Cornelia covered mounds at the Museum of Anthropology with plants grown by the indigenous people of the Pacific Northwest: grasses and wildflowers, fern (used for cough syrup), clover and vetch (used in medicines), mahonia (jellies and jams), and salmonberry and other berries (eaten or dried for use over the winter).

when research meant trips to libraries and resources that were sometimes on the other side of the continent, or even the world. "You don't have to be an expert in everything," she said. "You just need to know who the experts are, and when to go to them."

Of course, the aim with any project is to make it seem absolutely right that a building sits where it does. It should seem as if it has always been there, and *should* be there. "Achieving a fit between the built form and the land can only be done if all our design-related professions collaborate," Cornelia has said. "It's not just so the building and the land around it look good together. It is a matter of our planet's survival."

Landscape architect, James Taylor, has said, "Lots of other people – engineers, environmentalists, etc – can do pieces of work that landscape architects do, but they can't do the design, the big picture. Landscape architects are needed for that." Don Graham, another landscape architect, adds: "There's this 'little spark' that design professionals employ . . . You don't get it from a biologist. But a biologist and a landscape architect can work together to solve a problem like scum on a pond or birds not surviving."

The arts and skills of architect, engineer, and landscape architect truly support each other. But it isn't always a smooth ride. When Cornelia worked with architect, Moshe Safdie, on the National Gallery of Canada, Safdie wanted the land to slope a certain way; Cornelia had other ideas. Safdie claimed that the idea of using an A.Y. Jackson painting as a model for the landscape people would see as they climbed the ramp in the long atrium leading to the galleries was his; Cornelia said it was hers. Whenever creative minds sit down together to consider plans, it's often difficult to pinpoint precisely who came up with which ideas.

As with most professions, computers have changed the way many landscape architects do their work. There are programs that allow them to enter data about conditions at a site in order to simulate microclimates in three-dimensional models. Other programs allow them to look into the future, in a way, and see what a site might look like years down the road, when plants being considered have had a chance to mature.

Cornelia still does drawings by hand, but knows who to go to when computer-generated images are needed. She and fellow landscape architect Hank White commissioned microclimatic studies from the University of Guelph, when designing a courtyard for the fifty-four-story New York Times Building. The building's architect, Renzo Piano, was proposing that a birch grove should fill the entire courtyard. Solar maps provided by the university helped convince him to limit the birch grove to the northwest quadrant.

The miniature forest of tall birch trees and the undulating mounds covered with green moss in the less sunny part of the New York Times court-yard help connect people in the glass and steel skyscraper to nature and provide a tranquil respite in the midst of Manhattan's hustle and bustle. (Some aspects of the profession, like Cornelia's reason for practicing it, have not changed.)

For Cornelia, a project doesn't end once the building and landscaping are complete. Her supervision both during and after construction are essential.

One day she arrived at UBC's Museum of Anthropology and found a maintenance worker mowing the timothy, rye, and fescue grasses. "Excuse me, young man," she said. "Native people did not have lawn mowers. Why are you cutting the grass?" The grasses at the Museum of Anthropology were to be mowed only once a year – *after* they had gone to seed. If mowed more often, they would not flower.

c h a p t e r   f i f t e e n

The Art of the Possible

Despite frustrations, Cornelia loved her work. At seventy-five she was still involved in many projects, among them the creation of a master plan for ensuring that the 127-acre (51-hectare) campus of her alma mater, Smith College, would remain beautiful into the future. What an honor it was to be working where her hero, Frederick Law Olmsted, had worked one hundred years earlier.

Cornelia had returned to the school once before, to receive a Smith College Medal in 1982. When presenting the award, former Smith College president, Jill Ker Conway, (Smith's first female president) said, "Cornelia, it is your gift to solve with the eye of the artist the technical problems of bringing nature into easy relationships with steel and concrete. The daily routines of your fellow citizens bear witness, for you have changed their relationship to the buildings which surround them." Cornelia smiled. Unlike many people, this woman understood what she was about!

When Cornelia was first learning about landscape architecture, ecology was not even taught. Now it is an important part of all landscape architecture programs. "Landscape architects are looking at the land in a new way," Cornelia has said. "We used to plant just what we thought would make an

Cornelia designed a pond at the Museum of Anthropology in the 1970s to reflect changes in the sky and the importance of the sea creatures featured in the Haida art inside the museum. Opponents feared water would seep from the pond and speed erosion of the cliffs below. Cornelia lined the pond with bentonite clay so it would collect rainwater and possibly even slow erosion.

59

Cornelia's arguments about the pond she designed for the Museum of Anthropology site fell on deaf ears. It was filled on only two occasions – at the time of an APEC (Asia-Pacific Economic Cooperation) conference in 1997, and for the celebration of Arthur Erickson's eightieth birthday in 2004.

area beautiful, but that time is over. The planet need peacemakers, healers, and restorers: people with moral courage who will make our cities better places to live and who are willing to take risks in achieving it." The twentieth century also saw a shift from the making of fine gardens for the few who could afford them to beautifying public spaces around buildings, in national parks, and along parkways accessible to everyone.

As cities have grown, landscape architects have become involved in transforming waste spaces – like industrial waterfronts, highway underpasses, and derelict back alleys – into skate parks, animal habitats, and community gardens. Some landscape architects predict that as cities become more and more densely populated, as more and taller high-rises crowd closer to sidewalks and streets, and as green spaces get gobbled up by wider and faster roadways, people will need more places to reconnect with nature within their cities. Landscape architects will have to become experts at "the possibility of solitude."

The possibility of solitude. The possibility of healthy cities. The possibility of beautiful parks for everyone. The possibility of art and nature and humanity being one. *The art of the possible.*

And yet, Cornelia has had her complaints. "Bureaucracy. It stops you every five minutes. If you have innovative ideas, then you have to constantly invent ways and means, with research and examples, to convince people who aren't yet ready for change."

Nonetheless, well into her senior years, Cornelia continued to practice "the art of the possible" with Patience, Perseverance, Politeness – and two more "Ps" that she'd added to her arsenal: Professionalism and Passion. "They help get me through." Professionalism refers to Cornelia's technical competence, her inclination for research, her strong background in horticulture, and her ability to enhance an architect's ideas rather than imposing her own. Passion of course is that fiery spirit that fuels her drive to go on planting trees, building green roofs, and designing creative playgrounds; in other words, making the world around her and others a more beautiful and healthy place to be – for people and for the planet.

Kathy Stinson

Cornelia's wildest dream? "That cities will commit themselves to increasing the biomass – with more parks and community gardens where people can grow their own vegetables." How to achieve this dream? "More green roofs!"

Do you ever stop and think about why certain places make you feel the way they do? Landscape architects think about that sort of thing all the time. They know people are more likely to feel like sharing secrets in a small, enclosed space and to feel calm if they can see a horizon. They know that distances over open water seem shorter than the same distances over land, and that a downhill view seems longer than a view uphill. They know how to use light to make lines and shapes look sharper, or to blur them, and that you can make people notice an object just by placing it so it's seen in silhouette. They know that a curve in a pathway makes people want to follow the path to see what's beyond the curve.

chapter sixteen

More Spaces to Green

Cornelia was crazy about green roofs even before they became all the rage. You doubt green roofs are all the rage? During one week in April 2006, 11,629 people visited www.greenroofs.com, and visitors looked at almost double the number of pages on the site that month as they had a year before. In 1996, more than half the cities in Germany offered incentives to get people to install green roofs on their buildings. Laws in both Germany and Switzerland said that all new buildings *had* to have green roofs. Tokyo has set a target of 3,000 acres (roughly 1,200 hectares) of roof greenery by 2015. Cities in North America are looking into programs that will motivate more people to install green roofs, too.

Why Cornelia's enthusiasm and rising worldwide interest? The reasons are many.

Imagine stepping out onto the roof of a building and discovering a garden there. What better illustration of that element of surprise that Cornelia feels is so important in a landscape! "Secret gardens make us feel good," she says.

For Moshe Safdie's Vancouver Public Library building, Cornelia designed a roof garden in 1992 that she knew would be enjoyed by library workers and visitors, and even by people looking down on it from a nearby high-rise. A walkway would circle the library's top floor and perhaps become

An early model of the park-like roof garden Cornelia designed for the top of the new Vancouver Public Library building (opposite). Unfortunately, Cornelia's beautiful vision had to be scaled down because of budget cuts.

a favorite jogging path for library staff. A trellis covered with flowering vines would arch over part of a walkway. A waterfall would dampen urban noise and meadows of wildflowers would sway in the breeze. There would be an amphitheater and a "literary garden" to celebrate books with references to, say, roses. And at a small café people could buy lunch and lattés and take in the panoramic view of downtown. Cornelia imagined the roof becoming a favorite spot for concerts and weddings, with spillover crowds using escalators or elevators to reach outdoor patios on the floor below.

This lavish dream garden was never built. When the provincial government cut the budget for the new library, the first area to suffer was the accessible rooftop garden. A lot of people said, "Oh well, isn't Vancouver too rainy a city for a roof garden anyway?"

"No!" said Cornelia. "Our heavy rains are all the more reason to have as many green roofs here as possible, even if they are the kind that no one can visit!"

A roof garden no one could even visit? Was this woman nuts?

Cornelia was sent "back to the drawing board" to design a more affordable green roof, because even an inaccessible green roof made a lot of sense in terms of how it would benefit the environment. Why?

Ever notice how much better it feels to breathe in the country than in the city? That's not just because country air smells better (unless you're near a pig farm). Wherever there are more plants, the air contains more oxygen and less carbon dioxide and carbon monoxide. So green roofs improve the quality of a city's air. Plants filter airborne dust, too, and they absorb sound, so a building with a green roof is quieter inside than one with a hard roof. They also insulate the building against cold and heat, so the interior is more comfortable.

Ever notice that you feel hotter in the city than in the country? It's not your imagination. On infra-red satellite photos, cities show up as bright yellow globs in seas of cool green land. That's because brick, concrete, and glass all reflect a lot of the sun's heat into the air around them. Plants cool the air by absorbing heat – they need it to grow. So planting roof gardens reduces what scientists call the "urban heat island effect." Humans will benefit, and so will birds and insects, especially if plants that provide seeds and berries are used.

Incredible damage is done to the environment when developers replace fields and forests with buildings and roads. Green roof enthusiasts, like Cornelia, urge us to consider replacing vegetation lost to buildings by creating roof gardens, like this one on the Vancouver Public Library.

Websites like Google Earth are showing more and more people every day, through satellite images of our cities, the potential for green roof development.

Imagine a typical roof of a big shopping mall. Now imagine three to four feet (90 to 120 cm) of rain falling on that impervious roof every year. Almost all of that rainfall will run off into storm sewers. Sanitary sewers, which are separate from storm sewers, send sewage to treatment centers, *but* when there is more rainwater than the storm sewers can handle, the overflow combines with what's in the sanitary sewers and untreated sewage is sent into rivers, lakes, or the sea, depending on the city.

"Plant something on that roof, with proper growing medium, drainage system, and filter cloth," Cornelia said, "and it will hold onto 50 to 90 percent of the rain that lands on it. That's a lot of rain not going into sewers! And what does run off the roof will leave the roof slowly enough that the storm sewer won't overflow. The vegetation on the green roof will also absorb pollutants collected by the rain as it falls, which means less pollution in the waters where the runoff eventually ends up."

Still, there were skeptics. "That's a lot of rain you're asking the roof to hold onto. Won't there be leaks?" they asked.

"Not if you build it properly," said Cornelia. "Runoff will filter through a waffled core layer and be collected into drain pipes. And we will use also a rubberized membrane."

"All well and good," people continued to argue, "but what about the weight of all that extra water you're asking the roof to hold?"

"The roof will be built to take it."

But despite all the benefits of green roofs, some people still worry about their cost. Cornelia's answer? "Would you rather spend money on sewer systems and sewage treatment plants or on something that will help save our planet? And," she adds, knowing what some people care about most, "something that will add value to your property?" Cornelia would also point out, "Urban land is expensive. A rooftop is land you don't have to buy." The increased insulation a green roof provides also means saving on the cost of heating and air-conditioning, and roofing materials protected from the sun by gardens are cheaper to maintain than those taking the full impact of the sun's rays.

Cornelia advocates using city roof gardens to grow food, too, because food grown close to where it will be eaten is fresher. With less need for trucking, that also means a reduced toll on the environment and energy resources.

It's an idea that's catching on. Vancouver's Fairmont Waterfront Hotel has a green roof where thyme, rosemary, bay, wasabi, coriander, basil, and edible flowers are grown for use in the hotel's restaurant. In Toronto, a group called Foodshare is growing organic alfalfa, beans, clover, lentils, eggplant, herbs, and edible flowers on the roof of Annex Organics, for people in that community. The roof also has a fish pond stocked with tilapia.

The roof gardens Cornelia designed for Robson Square in the 1970s were not the first in North America, but they were considered among the most innovative on the continent. Cornelia may have felt like a pioneer when she first moved to Vancouver, but her involvement in the park-like green roof that emerged from her research for Robson meant she *was* a pioneer.

The green roof at Vancouver Library Square – built according to Cornelia's revised plan – became a model for green roof design in North America. After it was successfully completed, Public Works Canada commissioned Cornelia and two other architect/designers to write an Introductory Manual to Green Roofs, which is available online.

With more and more people buying into the idea of green roofs all the

time, their future looks good! The 2008 expansion of the Vancouver Convention Centre includes the largest green roof in Canada with six acres (2.4 hectares) of flowers and grasses. The Ford Motor Company's Rouge River truck plant in Dearborn, Michigan covers 10.4 acres (4.2 hectares)

The Vancouver library green roof was one of twenty-one projects in North America nominated for a Green Roofs Award of Excellence.

and absorbs four million gallons of rainwater each year. Renovations to the Jacob K. Javits Convention Center in New York will result in a twenty-two-acre (8.9-hectare) living roof in 2012. Other green roofs in North America include: Mountain Equipment Co-op's Toronto store, Chicago's city hall, and the Canadian Museum of Civilization in Hull, Quebec.

chapter seventeen

Seeds of the Future

Over the years, Cornelia has met with many groups of students and has arranged for visits to the British Columbia Institute of Technology's Green Roof Research Facility in Vancouver. In 2006, she urged the Canadian Centre for Architecture in Montreal to set up a program for children during an exhibit of her work there. The children would make "buildings" from milk cartons, cut to high-rise or cottage height as they wished, and create green roofs on them, using the same green roof materials that landscape architects and engineers would use. If there's one thing Cornelia is more passionate about than green roofs and healing our planet, it's educating young people so that they might come to share her passion!

Cornelia shares her love of plants with youngsters in the 1960s *(opposite)*. The children in the 1990s photo *(above)* are choosing what to plant on their green roofs.

🍂

Despite prestigious honors and ongoing landscaping projects, Cornelia's family was, as it always had been, key to her happiness. (By 2003 it had grown to include three granddaughters, Ariel, Talia, and Malka, and a grandson, Uri.) A page in Cornelia's daybook might show time set aside, amidst numerous meetings and presentations, to attend an all-candidates political meeting with her teenaged granddaughter, or to visit another granddaughter's allotment garden, to go skiing with her young grandson, or for a

This group of home-schooled young people is working on green roofs under Cornelia's direction at a visit to the British Columbia Institute of Technology.

session with her husband and their exercise coach.

Because Cornelia and Peter shared common professional goals, they talked about every work proposal – hers or his – that ever left their house. Sometimes they even worked together on projects, as they had on their first date. When either had work that took them away from Vancouver, they often traveled together.

After returning home from a United Nations conference in Turkey in 1996, Cornelia wrote a letter to her grandchildren. In it, she quoted the nineteenth-century Russian writer, Fyodor Dostoyevsky, and told them that his words had often given her courage:

> Love all creation, both the whole and every grain of sand. Love every leaf, every ray of light, all animals. If you love everything, you will perceive the mystery in all, and when you perceive this, you will grow every day in fuller understanding of it, until you come at last to love the whole world with a love that will be all-embracing and universal.

Peter Oberlander was the first Canadian to obtain a master of city planning degree. For his work in urban planning, he was named a member of the Order of Canada. He has also been an architect, a citizenship judge for British Columbia and the Yukon, and a university professor. When he retired from teaching, he continued to act as a consultant on human settlements, nationally and internationally.

Cornelia did love the whole world – well, maybe not the bureaucrats who stood in the way of some of her dreams – and she recognized that there are many ways of making a difference in the world. As her ancestors had provided role models for her in the first half of the twentieth century, so did she and Peter for their offspring.

Kathy Stinson

A strong work ethic, a social conscience, creativity, and love of the environment, research, and of children, are all apparent in the career paths each of their grown children has chosen. Judy has worked to preserve heritage buildings and as a Director for the City Program at British Columbia's Simon Fraser University. Tim is a pediatrician whose research led him to co-edit a book called *Pain in Children and Adults with Developmental Disabilities*. Wendy is an artist, an award-winning filmmaker, and teacher.

chapter eighteen

A Garden Lost, a Garden Found

In 1998, Cornelia received an invitation from the German government to return there as their guest, along with others who had been forced to leave the country in the 1930s and '40s. When her daughter Wendy suggested she accept the invitation, Cornelia responded matter-of-factly, "Why should I go to Germany as a Jew when I did not live there as a Jew?"

There was also a certain sense of 'You didn't want me then, why should I want you now?' in her reluctance to go. But what an incredible push-pull the dilemma produced. In the years since Cornelia had left and turned her back on all that had happened there, Berlin had sat far in the background. How could she return? And yet . . .

It was asparagus season when Cornelia returned to Berlin with her daughter in 1998. The house she had lived in as a girl had been subdivided for four families to live in.

Wendy insisted that they go and look at Cornelia's childhood home. They went to Bernhard Beyerstrasse No. 3. At the garden gate through which she had watched her family's furniture carried by the Nazis, Cornelia pointed out to Wendy the purple lilac that her mother had planted. It was in bloom, but the garden was badly overgrown.

Over the roar of traffic, Cornelia said loudly, "That's where we used to cut through the woods. And over there is where my friend Jutta lived. She

73

lived in hiding for five years and later came to America."

Going back to Germany and her childhood garden, Cornelia felt as if she were in a movie, or "in borrowed shoes too large" for her. She told Wendy about the purse she had buried, and even showed her where, but "none if it felt real."

Wendy asked, "Shall we dig up the purse now?"

"No," Cornelia said. "Someone has probably taken it."

And perhaps someone had. Or perhaps Cornelia had buried, with that purse, all memory of what it had meant to have to leave the country of her birth – her enchanted garden – and all these years later, she wasn't about to dig up any of it. Not when she felt, as she told Wendy on their return to Canada, "My roots are not in Europe, they are in the new world, with my husband and family and friends and my work. How lucky I was to come so early in my life to North America, to have the opportunity to create what I have . . . I am just so grateful."

Soon after, Wendy made a film about their visit and the history behind it. Wendy says in the film (called *Stille*), "The ability to forget is a gift."

It seems fitting and a touch ironic – remarkable, certainly – that on the brink of the twenty-first century, Cornelia was asked to design the landscape for the new Canadian embassy in Berlin, at No. 17 Leipziger Platz, with Kuwabara Paine Bloomberg Architects.

The property had once belonged to the prominent, Jewish-owned department store chain, Wertheim, but when the Nazi Party took it over in 1937, it became the wartime office of Germany's propaganda minister, Joseph Goebbels. Immediately south of No. 17 had sat the headquarters of the most dreaded institutions of Hitler's Third Reich: the Gestapo, the Security Service, and the Reich Security. There they had planned the extermination of all German and European Jews, and detained, tortured, or killed opponents of Hitler's policies. Just north of Leipziger Platz lay the remains of the bunker where Hitler committed suicide in 1945, and a network of tunnels that had housed his SS guard.

Canada's flag waves atop the Canadian embassy in Berlin. Beneath the flag in Cornelia's green roof wends a river of glass inspired by one of Canada's great rivers.

Never one to dwell on the past, Cornelia got down to the business she'd been hired for. With her concept of symbolically tying the two countries together in mind, she flipped through a file of photographs. She knew what she was looking for. She had flown over it on trips to Europe.

Here it was. An aerial photo of the Mackenzie River delta in Canada's north, glistening with light. Could she replicate its beauty on the roof of the Canadian embassy in Berlin?

Putting together her artistic intelligence and technical know-how, Cornelia made her plans. She sketched the shape of a river meandering through a landscape that would be planted with – Cornelia's heart beat faster as she recognized her best choice – kinnikinnick, the hardy, green ground-cover that grows from coast to coast in Canada and that she had used in many of her Canadian landscape designs.

Perhaps influenced by the blue River Rhine in the city plan on the wall of the studio where she'd had her portrait painted almost seventy years before,

Cornelia planned on filling the "riverbed" with blue glass pebbles. As she was rolling one between her palms, it suddenly occurred to her that if she intended the glass river to reflect the sky that links Canada and Germany, then only black pebbles would do.

"It is a piece of art," Cornelia said during the planning stages, "but it will also drain all the rain water into a cistern in the basement that holds 224,000 liters of water. That water will then be cleaned with ultraviolet rays for use in the toilets." Like other roof gardens she had created, the one atop the embassy would be an ecological marvel.

In the end, no pebbles were used in the rooftop riverbed. Due to budget restrictions, less expensive, glass tiles (black) were used instead. Not as beautiful as what Cornelia had envisioned, but the simulation of one of Canada's majestic rivers on German soil is nonetheless a wonderful emblem for the kind of global community she believes in.

That Cornelia could absorb the Holocaust into her experience, return to the city that had rejected her, and – through her passion for creating landscapes – transform that expulsion into something beautiful, useful, and connected to nature . . . Is it any wonder this woman speaks so confidently and so passionately of "the art of the possible"?

chapter nineteen

And into the 21st Century

Cornelia punched her poles into the snow and pushed off from a high peak at Blackcomb Mountain in the Canadian Rockies. Cold wind nipped her face as she picked up speed. Almost eighty years old, she still loved the sensations she'd first known as a young girl hurtling down ski hills in Switzerland – the smell of the snow, the tensing and relaxing of muscles to guide her skis, the sparkle of flakes flying up behind other skiers. Now, she often took Fridays off in winter to go skiing with her husband and grandchildren. One day in 2000, as she sailed down a slope, she saw brilliant sun reflecting off an ice patch. And then she hit it.

Cornelia regained consciousness in the Vancouver General Hospital – in the Burns and Plastics Surgery unit. Her broken sinus had been replaced with a new plastic one.

From her bed, she stared out at a bleak concrete terrace, longing for the lush greenery outside her bedroom window at home. Patients who had suffered burns would be stuck here for much longer than she would, she realized. For many long, painful weeks they would have nothing green and natural to look at.

Knowing that the better people feel, the better they heal, she said to herself, 'This is terrible. Something must be done.'

When drawing up her plans for a healing garden – with the help of her

Cornelia donated her time and skills to design a lightly shaded, rooftop patio garden for patients at the Vancouver General Hospital.

77

Cornelia's fondness for
mounds comes through
again in the landscaping
at King David High School
in Vancouver.

long-time assistant Elisabeth Whitelaw (a landscape architect herself) and some students of landscape architecture at UBC – Cornelia was aware that a person sitting or lying down experiences a garden differently from someone who is standing. Among flowering magnolia trees and clematis vines, she placed a small fountain. To burn victims, the soothing sound of trickling water is especially significant because it's often what saved their lives.

❦

In the spring of 2001, a friend suggested throwing a big party to celebrate Cornelia's eightieth birthday, but "The Grande Dame: a design legend with staying power" (as *Gardening Life* magazine would call her a few years later) didn't want anyone making a fuss. She didn't mind being the center of attention if the focus was on ideas she believed in – like the benefits of nature, or concern for the environment – but to have the spotlight on her personally? No thank you. Cornelia chose instead to gather a small group of friends for a quiet picnic outdoors, and, as she did every year with her family, to celebrate the arrival of another summer.

Cornelia was still busy attending meetings, fighting bureaucracies, designing landscapes (her c.v. lists involvement in no fewer than seven major projects in 2001). On into her eighties, her landscape projects included a mixed income housing community in Seattle with a central park and market garden; Wellesley Central Place Park in Toronto; courtyard gardens at the New York Times Building; and in Vancouver a residential garden, a play area at a family resource center, the healing garden at the hospital, and an educational landscape at King David High School, using plants mentioned in the bible. She also helped develop the botanical garden at the Hebrew University of Jerusalem. Cornelia was offering friends and acquaintances advice on their education and careers too, introducing them to other design professionals, and traveling to deliver speeches. Solutions to problems threatening the health of our planet had become a regular subject of her presentations.

"Between the early years of my career and the present," Cornelia said to an audience of hundreds who came to the Toronto Botanical Garden to hear her

speak in 2005, "problems like global warming, depletion of the ozone, and the toxicity of our air, land, and water have increasingly threatened the health of our planet, causing problems for thousands of Earth's inhabitants – energy shortages (brownouts and high fuel costs), tidal flooding, increased rates of skin cancer and of other illnesses resulting from exposure to pollutants. Not to mention all the havoc wreaked upon the habitats of birds and other animals . . ."

To audiences of landscape architects all over North America, she said, "We must use techniques that will help us survive into the next century . . . Landscape architects, architects, and engineers have a critical role to play in mitigating the impact of the environmental degradation of our planet – ozone depletion, global warming, resource reduction, indoor and outdoor pollution. These cannot be seen as problems too big to address."

In 2004, Cornelia represented the Canadian Society of Landscape Architects (of which she had been president in 1987) at the World Urban Forum meetings in Barcelona, Spain. "Don't think of me as a European," she has said. "I am really an American product with a knapsack full of culture." Cornelia had become an American citizen in 1944 and a Canadian citizen in 1962, but in fact she considered herself a global citizen – a citizen of the planet.

There are 80,000 landscape architects worldwide. Since the profession is partly an artistic endeavor, their outdoor spaces can be as varied as landscape paintings. Of course most do contain plant materials, but gardens designed by Mia Guttfreund Lehrer, originally from El Salvador, also contain quirky combinations of pottery and other objects. When American Martha Schwartz designed the grounds for an insurance company in Munich, Germany, she arranged geometrical beds of glass, stone, and plastic around the building. Canadian Claude Cormier covered a diseased tree slated for removal from someone's California property with 100,000 blue balls. Some people loved it and others hated it, but it became an international symbol of "bold and savvy" landscape design.

chapter twenty

Home

A t Jim Everett Park in Vancouver, a teenaged boy kicks a soccer ball to his teammate on the other side of an oval-shaped playing field. His girlfriend sits on a concrete retaining wall that circles the grassy area. She is babysitting two children, who are climbing a hill at the far end of the field, loudly counting the boulder steps as they climb.

The little girl beats her brother to the top. "Come look," she yells.

On the other side of the hill is a pond.

"Wow!" the boy shouts, and the children run down the hill. To catch up with them, the babysitter follows a path around the base of the mound. The long-needled pines in the park remind her of the wind-swept trees at her grandparents' cottage in Ontario. So do the birch trees that grow on the long, low hill that separates the park from the street.

At the pebbled edge of the pond, the children have already begun to invent a game – gathering sticks and stones, sorting them into piles, and throwing some category of rejects into the water.

When the teenaged boy's soccer game ends, he goes to the rose garden and with his penknife cuts a blossom from one of the bushes. He pockets the knife and takes the flower to his girlfriend. Before they take the children home and head to his dad's place for supper in the apartment building nearby, he brushes

A young girl takes in the view from atop the mound at Cornelia's Jim Everett Park in Vancouver.

Spring, when the apple trees are in blossom, is an especially beautiful time – for the nose as well as the eyes. Landscape architects aim to engage the senses when they design parks.

a butterfly from his girlfriend's shoulder. An elderly gentleman strolling by with his dog watches the young couple wistfully.

Cornelia loves watching people use the beautiful urban park she helped create. "It's a twenty-first century park," she says, "because principles of ecological sensitivity underlie its design, it is affordable, low maintenance, and it's a place all kinds of people are comfortable to visit."

Few if any of the park's visitors give even a passing thought to what went into transforming the site into what it is now.

To, improve drainage, soil had to be scraped off the area that would become the playing field. Since trucking it away would be both expensive and polluting, Cornelia instead had it moved to form the low long mound along the busy street side of the park and the larger "King of the Castle" mound in the middle.

Recycled bricks for the paved area were laid over sand so that the rainwater could return to the earth. Drainage tile was placed under the playing field to collect runoff that had originally made the area soggy. This runoff now flows into a pipe that extends under the playing field, under the big hill, and into the wetland beyond.

It's hard to believe that Jim Everett Park was once a flat, soggy, triangular patch of ground that most people wouldn't even notice as they whizzed by in cars or on bikes.

In the gravel around the pond, irises, sedge, skunk cabbage, and rushes were planted. The beautiful Japanese plum trees planted on the site forty years ago were saved and new birch trees were added – on the low mound and at the entrance to the park.

Kathy Stinson

At eighty-five Cornelia still believes that traditional playground equipment does little to encourage children's creativity. At Jim Everett Park, landforms encourage children to be creative and to become absorbed in the games they make up. The pond is just deep enough to puddle around in without being dangerous. The hill inspires whole geographies and the acting out of countless stories. Bushes provide good places to hide from grownups who sit chatting on nearby benches.

The paths through the park are granular, not paved, so that water can seep through them. No water from Jim Everett Park drains into the storm sewer system. The only grass that needs mowing is on the mounds and it needs to be mown only once a year, after the seeds of the wildflowers have dropped. Most of the trees and plants are native species, so they do well without any special attention.

As she did at the National Gallery years before, Cornelia used misshapen pines at this park because she prefers the beauty of more natural-looking trees to that of "perfect" nursery trees. (They also cost a fraction of what perfectly shaped trees do.) The rocks that form steps climbing up the hill came from nearby. "It's amazing what you can do even with a small budget," Cornelia says. "Often all that's missing is the will."

A child rolls down the grassy hill, laughing.

"You know," Cornelia says to her companion, "I've been involved with a lot of projects, but the playgrounds still hold for me a special place."

It saddens her to know that many of them would not be built today because people are too worried about being sued if a child were to get hurt. Still, landscape architecture's interest in children's playgrounds continues. "There's a professional journal called *Landscapes/Paysages*," Cornelia says. "The Spring 2005 issue was entirely devoted to children's landscapes. You should read it."

The issue acknowledges that life is even more structured and constrained for children now than it was in the 1960s and '70s, and that opportunities for children to take risks and be creative are often designed out of play spaces.

In any season trees can be important in making a building appear comfortable on its site.

Landscape architect Don Hester said in one article, "Children need unstructured opportunities to express their creativity. Perhaps cuts, scrapes and broken bones have to be considered part of the normal growing-up experience. Maybe current concerns about overweight kids (because they are focused on the excitement of video games) would diminish if [the kids] could do more fun things in the real world." In another article, Susan Herrington, associate professor of landscape architecture and environmental design at UBC and a specialist in outdoor spaces for children, said, "As landscape architects we are uniquely equipped to capture the thrill and wonder of the outdoors in the landscapes we design for children."

Cornelia's advice for playground designers? "Watch children. Watch how they play. Dream how you'd like them to grow. Give them the chance to develop their muscles, minds, spirit, and social graces. And think about how to adapt tried-and-true ideas to our times."

"In a garden we have indeed left the real world and entered the world of fantasy and make-believe, where nature, under the control of art, gives pleasure and rest and escape from today's worries." – Humphrey Carver

Back at Cornelia's Vancouver home, we stroll through her garden. She brushes her hand over the feathery head of a clump of ornamental grass. "It is not only possible that our cities not be concrete jungles," she says, "it is essential for our survival." As she considers Jim Everett Park a twenty-first century park, so she considers her own garden a twenty-first century garden. It provides privacy and nature in a small space, it needs little water, and it's low maintenance. Its design, conceived more than thirty-five years ago, was ahead of its time. It was then, and still is now, a garden for the future.

Conclusion

Many people retire in their sixties or seventies, but well into her eighties, Cornelia had no intention of calling it quits. Did she feel she needed to make the most of her life because she might well have lost it if her family had stayed in Germany? When I asked her, she said, "Of course."

Cornelia may well have felt driven, as many Holocaust survivors did, to earn the chance at life that she'd been given. And to prove – especially to herself – that she deserved that chance.

But the truth is also that Cornelia simply loves her work.

"The greatest satisfaction is to be creative. Every day I jump out of bed because I enjoy it . . . It's also tremendously satisfying to have people come, see what you've done, and go away wanting to do it themselves."

The idea of becoming a landscape architect may have taken hold of Cornelia when she saw the city plan on the wall of a portrait painter's studio. But I think that the essence of what has kept her at her profession for sixty-plus years is to be found in these words that Cornelia has delivered to audiences all over the world: "If we join others in effective leadership to create the 'Global Garden,' who knows, we may even realize the ever-longed for Garden of Eden."

Did the expulsion from her garden in Germany shape the kind of work Cornelia would do and how she would approach it? I think so. I would even dare to say that Cornelia may have been striving throughout her career to recreate her own "Garden of Eden." (Interestingly, "garden" means "paradise" in Persian.)

I am certain Cornelia would say to this theory, "Nonsense, Kathy. It's love of the land – of nature – that makes me do this work. Let's just leave it at that."

Whatever fires this woman's passion to make urban spaces greener, there is no doubt that cities are more beautiful as a result of her work, and city-dwellers' hectic lives are much improved. The world is a better place for Cornelia's having been in it.

Kathy Stinson

In 2006, the Canadian Society of Landscape Architecture presented Cornelia with a Lifetime Achievement Award, the first such award the organization had given.

I wish Cornelia many more years of "jumping out of bed" to continue the work she so loves.

Cornelia juggles apples from a tree planted in her garden when her children were young as well as she does all aspects of her remarkable life.

acknowledgments

How do I begin to thank all the people who helped with this project in some way? Peter Carver and Peter Oberlander; Cornelia Oberlander and Elisabeth Whitelaw; others in the Oberlander family, and especially those I had the pleasure to meet, Judy, Wendy, Ariel, and Uri; the Landscape Architecture Canada Foundation, and especially Faye Langmaid; Holly McNally, Sarah Pypker, Theo Heras, Joanne Stanbridge; the Canadian Society of Landscape Architects, and especially members Cecilia Paine, Fran Pauze, Adrienne Brown, Macklin Hancock, Cynthia Girling, Alexander Budrevics, and Humphrey Carver; Arthur Erickson, Steven Cox; Matthias Wiesmann, Elisabeth Brunner; Ainslie and David Manson, Janet and Scott Barclay, Blair Kerrigan; Rae Fleming, Linda Granfield, Frieda Wishinsky, Michael Cox; Emily Bowerman; staff of the Toronto Botanical Gardens, and especially Cathie Cox and Graham Curry; staff of the Canadian Centre for Architecture, and especially Robert Desaulniers, Giovanna Borasi, and Anne-Marie Sigouin; Lorna Rourke, Scott Heaney; Vicky Gabereau and Peter Gzowski, on tape; Ian McHarg (*Design with Nature*), Witold Rybczinski (*A Clearing in the Woods*), Daphne Bramham (*The Vancouver Sun*); Max Kerrigan, Wendy Angus, Jamie Bastedo, Jon Downey; Sharon Butala; Lena Coakley, Hadley Dyer, and Paula Wing; and the staff at Tundra and especially Carolyn Jackson, Jennifer Lum, Kathryn Cole, Lauren Bailey, Claire Sharpe, and Kathy Lowinger.

photo credits

Front Cover: Kathy Stinson

Page 1: Kathy Stinson

Page 13: Kathy Stinson

Page 20: Kathy Stinson

Page 27: Malak Photographs

Page 28: Malak Photographs

Pages 34, 35: Kathy Stinson

Page 36: Peter Carver

Page 38: Peter Carver

Page 41: Kiku Hawkes

Page 47: Kathy Stinson

Page 63: Kathy Stinson

Page 65: Kathy Stinson

Page 84: Peter Carver

Page 86: Kathy Stinson

Page 87: Kiku Hawkes

All other photos and drawings are from the personal
and professional collections of Cornelia Hahn Oberlander and of her family.
Many of the professional photos were taken by Elisabeth Whitelaw.